Success in Reading and Writing: Grade 4

The Textbook Concept of the Future

D0856107

ADDITIONAL TITLES IN THE SUCCESS IN READING AND WRITING SERIES

Success in Kindergarten Reading and Writing
Anne H. Adams, Mary Johnson, Judith Connors

Success in Beginning Reading and Writing
Anne H. Adams

Phonics/Spelling Activity Sheets for use with Success in Beginning Reading and Writing

Success in Reading and Writing, Grade Two
Anne H. Adams and Helen Cappleman

Success in Reading and Writing, Grade Five
Anne H. Adams, Jean Bernholz, Pat Sumner

Success in Reading and Writing, Grade Six
Anne H. Adams and Elizabeth Bebensee

Success in Reading and Writing: Grade 4

The Textbook Concept of the Future

Anne H. Adams

Patricia Horne Sumner

Jean F. Bernholz

Good Year Books • Santa Monica, California

Library of Congress Cataloging in Publication Data

Adams, Anne H.
  Success in reading and writing, grade four.

  Includes bibliographies and index.
    1. Language arts (Elementary) 2. English lan-
guage—Study and teaching (Elementary) 3. Fourth
grade (Education) I. Sumner, Patricia Horne.
II. Bernholz, Jean F. III. Title.
LB1576.A387 1982   372.6   81-6401
ISBN 0-673-16545-0   AACR2

ISBN: 0-673-16545-0

Copyright © 1982 Anne H. Adams, Patricia Horne Sumner, Jean F. Bernholz.

All Rights Reserved.

Printed in the United States of America.

4 5 6-BKC-88 87

Dedicated
to
Dorris Baird
who was there

and to
the late Anne H. Adams

Contents

Preface

The keys to teaching reading and writing have always been, are now, and will always be (1) the teacher, and (2) what is taught.

At the upper elementary level, the intelligence, educational background, and expertise of teachers should be foremost in curriculum implementation. Students are curious, interested, and open to expansion of their knowledge in limitless topics. Unfortunately, in some schools, professional teachers are spending precious planning or instruction time checking boxes on skill sheets, running stencils, or performing other clerical chores. A college graduate has much more to offer elementary students. The *Success* program frees the teacher to teach and students to learn.

There are many different kinds of "textbooks" to use as reading materials in the classroom. Some are bound in the traditional mode of the science, mathematics, and social studies content books. Others come in the form of newspapers, and change content each day. Still others appear as magazines, pamphlets, reference books, and so on. The *Success* program introduces a broader concept of the textbook than the traditional one.

Especially during the past two decades, apprehension about reading instruction has abounded. The public has screamed for more effectiveness; educators have chronicled problems, researched theories, and published numerous materials in search of a solution. Legislatures and school districts have poured millions of dollars into purchasing new equipment and brightly colored packages hoping for a panacea.

Unfortunately, these efforts, though filled with good intent, have created additional problems in the classroom. Teachers have been expected somehow to find time to incorporate these ever-changing ideas, materials, and organizational patterns into their instructional program. For example, recent theories on how to "individualize" instruction have resulted in teachers having to plan several lessons daily for the same teaching time, incorporate several programs, and make use of many materials ranging from comprehension kits to audiovisual machines. To do so, teachers have had to group their students for instruction according to abilities, or unfortunately in some instances, according to which students in the class had not completed a given page in a workbook. Essentially, in some schools, the urgency to use the products was given priority over the process.

Despite public criticism and falling test scores, there have remained many good teachers who, although at times discouraged, have not deserted the concept of professionalism. It is only with these teachers and sound educational programs that successful reading and writing instruction will become a widespread reality.

In order to return control of teaching to the teacher working with students, some of the practices which have been proven ineffective for all students and have burdened teachers must disappear from the classroom. It is time to combine common sense and educationally sound practices to bring to teacher and students the respect they have so long deserved.

Attention, time, and money need to be directed toward a planned approach that gets the mundane out of the way so that teachers can teach students to read, or attempt to read, newspapers, fiction, and nonfiction library books, content area textbooks, labels, maps, magazines, reference books, etc. without fear. We do not need a generation of people who can or cannot labor through basal stories, complete a card in a kit, or fill in blanks in a workbook. In fact, running another stencil may be compounding the problem rather than solving it. We need a generation of elementary students who are avid, comfortable readers of almost anything in print.

We are moving, fortunately, away from the idea that a panacea exists. We realize that individualized instruction means just that—a few seconds or minutes between teacher and individual student concerning exactly what that student is doing, has done, or should be doing academically.

Our generation can be the first to experience amazing and exciting continuity and growth in the reading, writing, and self-concepts of its youth. We know what has happened to students and teachers in the past. To change the experience to massive numbers of students who *can* read and who *want to* read will not happen by accident. Fortunately, in this country we do have professional teachers, supervisors, and administrators whose expertise will provide students with a textbook concept of the future.

The perspective of the *Success in Reading and Writing* program moves far beyond associating a person's reading ability or "level" with a traditionally graded set of books. In the program described in this book *anything in print within reason is considered a textbook and part of the program*.

The *Success* program introduces the concept of extensive, in-depth reading/writing instruction with the overall intent to promote growth of knowledge while developing reading and writing abilities, rather than piecemeal reading of stories and isolated skills activities. In this process, teachers are freed to teach and to use fully the humanities, social sciences, physical sciences, art and information gained through their many years of education. Many traditional teachers' editions are so binding that they tell the teacher, a college graduate, the exact word to say when teaching a lesson and, in essence, control the teacher.

The *Success* program endorses the idea that teachers can teach and students can learn when the avenues for teaching and learning are *open and flexible* rather than restricted. This program presents a base structure that encourages flexibility so that any teacher can develop the structure according to his or her expertise and according to the students in the class. To further expedite the process of improving students' reading and writing abilities, writing instruction is closely linked to reading instruction in the modules.

The *Success* concepts of associating anything in print as a part of an umbrella reading program, emphasizing growth of knowledge along with the development of reading/writing skills, and faith in teachers to combine process with product, was piloted during 1977–78 at the first grade level[1] in the Durham, North Carolina City Schools. At the end of that year, these inner city students averaged at the 74th percentile,[2] 24 points *above* the national average, rather than at the 23rd percentile, where the previous average had fallen. The positive *had* taken place; students who were not supposed to be able to read and write independently *were* doing just that.

During the piloting of the *Success in Beginning Reading and Writing* program in the first grades, parents and educators expressed a need for the concepts of the first-level *Success* program to be continued and expanded into the next grades. They wanted an elimination of stilted, stereotyped program components that might erase much of the educational gain and enjoyment of reading and writing that these first graders had experienced. Kindergarten, second, and third grade *Success* classes were piloted during 1977–78.

Success in Reading and Writing programs for grades four, five, and six were piloted during 1978–79 in Hillsborough, Durham, Charlotte, and Greensboro, North Carolina and in Charleston, South Carolina. The program was found to be effective in teaching persons who cannot read and write independently as well as average and gifted readers/writers. Although designed originally for use in regular classrooms, the program has been adapted easily and used in remedial reading classes, including adult classes for bilingual education and in classes for emotionally disturbed students. The program has been taught in both private and public schools.

1. See *Success in Beginning Reading and Writing: The Basal Concept of the Future* by Anne H. Adams, Goodyear Publishing Company, 1978.
2. Comprehensive Tests of Basic Skills, CTB/McGraw Hill.

The *Success* program is a structured yet flexible management system for teachers to use, based on a belief in the expertise of professional teachers to use a skeleton outline of a balanced reading/writing program and adapt it to the individual student's growth process. The *Success* program scraps the jargon, eliminates stereotyping of students, and removes tangible and intangible obstacles to growth of communication skills and knowledge. It signals a new day of respect for what happens in the schools.

This program may not appeal initially to those who are conditioned to expect less than the best from teachers and students. It will encourage those educators who are not satisfied with the emphasis on watered-down educational content at the expense of excellence in learning and in teaching because it provides an alternative.

The number of teaching hours does not change each year. What can change is what is done during the instructional time. This program borrows from the best ideas of the past and projects a better educational future.

Anne H. Adams
Patricia Horne Sumner
Jean F. Bernholz

Acknowledgments

Grateful appreciation is expressed to the following people whose assistance/encouragement helped to make this book a reality:

To Anne Flowers, Dean, School of Education, Georgia Southern College; R. Mike Simmons, Superintendent of Orange County Schools; Benjamin T. Brooks, Superintendent of Brunswich County Schools; Kenneth R. Newbold, Superintendent of Greensboro City Schools; Jay Robinson, Superintendent of Charlotte/Mecklenburg Schools in North Carolina; and Robert Johnston, Headmaster, University School of Milwaukee, Wisconsin; John H. McInnis, retired Principal of Grady Brown School in Orange County; Dennis Nichols, Principal of Morehead School and Calvin Morgan, Principal of Glenn School in Durham; Lois Carver, Principal of Marie Davis School, Ralph Cline, Principal of Sterling School; Larry Sides, Principal of Newell School, Charles Sigmon, Principal of Winterfield School in Charlotte; Pat Neal, Principal of Red Springs Elementary School; Charles G. Clark, Superintendent of Education, Hawaii; Kenneth Yamamoto, Chief Planner for Reading for the State of Hawaii; Roberta Tokumaru, Curriculum Consultant, Frances Shimotsu, District Educational Specialist for Hawaii; Kathryn Gilliam, Member of the School Board, Ellen Carnes, Instructional Facilitator K-3, Alfred Roberts, Principal of Dunbar School, and Betty Perkins, Coordinator, in the Dallas, Texas Independent Schools; Joyce Wasdell, Assistant Superintendent for Instruction, Robert Moffett, Head of the Lower and Middle Schools, Betty Russell, Director of Studies, Richard E. Wilke, School Psychologist, and Susan Craig, Director of Reading in the University School of Milwaukee; Vincent Reed, Superintendent of Schools, James Guines, Assistant Superintendent of Instruction, Teresa Posey, Regional Superintendent, William Saunders, Region Superindent, Mary Harris, Supervisor in the Washington, D.C., schools; Barry Munson, Director of Reading, Halifax County Schools; Carol Johnson, Director of Curriculum, Bloomfield Hills, Michigan.

To the following teachers who worked closely with the authors in developing and/or piloting the program:

Judy Alford, Mamie Alston, Barbara Collins and Susan Warren in the Durham City Schools; Greg Wagoner in Whiteland, Indiana; Rosetta Burrell, Joan Curry, Ann Dillon, Lynette Harvey, Clara P. Martin and Eulane Byrd in the Durham County Schools; Donna Jacobs in Dallas, Texas; Pat Adkisson, Emily Bearden, Lucille Brown, Margaret Claiborne, Marilyn Gehner, Betty Hollifield, Catherine Holman. Lelia Lindsay, Flossie Rich, Carolyn Simms, and Linda Kay Tyler in the Charlotte/Mecklenburg Schools; Nancy Tamanaha in Hawaii; Barbara Gottesman, Joann Gresso and Roberta Pearson in the Greensboro City Schools; Janet Schneider in Louisville, Kentucky.

To the following persons who took the time to observe some of the classes and/or whose comments encouraged the authors to continue working on the program concept:

The Honorable Terry Sanford, President of Duke University and former Governor of North Carolina; Robert Pittillo, Associate Chairman of the Department of Education at Duke University; The Honorable James Green, Lieutenant Governor of North Carolina; Craig Phillips, State Superintendent of Public Instruction in North Carolina; Mary Purnell, Director and Betty Jean Fause, Assistant Director of the Division of Reading in the North Carolina State Department of Public Instruction; The Honorable Charles Campbell, Educator and Senator, State of Hawaii; Alton Cheek, Principal, Louis Martin, Reading Teacher and Katie Brown, Teacher at Efland-Cheeks School in Hillsborough, North Carolina; Ina Tabibian and Chris Jennison, Goodyear Publishing Company; The Honorable Willis Witchard and Kenneth Royall, Senators in the North Carolina Legislature; Steed Rollins, Publisher, Cornelia Olive, Reporter, *The Durham Sun*, and Barbara Siebel, Newspaper in Education Coordinator for including some of the letters to the editor written by students in editions of the *Sunshine Special*; Mick Hauver of *The Washington Post*; Betty Debnam, Editor of *The Mini Page*; James Sawyer, Director of Membership and Council Relations, International Reading Association; Judith Hines, Manager of Educational Services, American Newspaper Publishers Association Foundation; Glenn Keever, Editor, *North Carolina Education*; the interns at the Duke University Reading Center who taught many of the lessons prior to their use in the schools; to graduate students who helped edit, proofread and develop lessons, Jane Clunie, David Malone and Mark Smylie; Robert Booth and James Maxwell of the Durham Chamber of Commerce; and the students who provided the information found on the charts and student writings in the book.

Success in Reading and Writing: Grade 4

The Textbook Concept of the Future

chapter one

Getting Ready to Teach the Program

THE TEXTBOOK CONCEPT OF THE FUTURE

The *Success* program introduces the concept of *the textbook of the future*—an unlimited wealth of information from educators, parents, businesses, resources from other parts of the nation and world, and from the students. A traditional subject textbook is viewed as only one source of information to be used by students in learning about a topic or theme. The language arts block of the *Success* program incorporates reading and content area textbooks, but only as parts, rather than as major emphases of improving reading, writing, speaking, listening, and thinking skills.

The concept of the textbook of the future, as presented in this book, views any printed information within reason—newspapers, coupons, encyclopedias, textbooks from different publishers on different "levels," library books, words on television screens, thesauruses, etc.—as part of the student's textbook materials. Using these materials for teaching reading and writing and improving thinking skills can be far more exciting and interesting than any canned material with multiple robotlike copies. Instead of being concerned about whether a student can read a certain "graded" basal reader or content area textbook on a certain "grade level," we should be concerned about whether that student can read a variety of books, magazine stories, content area information from numerous printed sources, newspapers, and so on.

Students have approximately 180 days in each of the upper elementary grades to improve their communication skills in an educational setting. The growth these students can experience between day one and day 180 within a grade level should not be underestimated. Students in upper elementary grades do have the ability and eagerness to read and write about a variety of topics. The reading/writing program must provide them with those opportunities.

Students progressing into the upper elementary grades encounter an increase in the amount and depth of printed information they receive. Content area materials available in the classroom provide some of this information. Exposure to television, newspapers, magazines, library books, dictionaries, and other reference materials also helps students develop an awareness of current events and helps them expand their vocabulary and conceptual development around a myriad of topics. All of these valuable resources should be included as integral parts of the instructional program. This is a change from the approach that endorses a small number of books and workbooks as the backbone of the instructional program during an academic year.

Until such time as we have provided classes with at least an adequate number of magazine subscriptions, newspapers, content area textbooks containing various reports of the same major topics for study, paper, and the like, we should not give priority to tax

1

monies for basal and supplementary "reading books" and ancillary materials. Instead of purchasing the same science, social studies, and mathematics textbooks for the same grade level, we should be introducing students to information in a variety of sources, including a variety of content area textbooks. We may achieve greater results once we depart from traditional purchasing techniques.

THE BASIC ASSUMPTION

Success in Reading and Writing: Grade 4 expands student knowledge in the humanities, social sciences, physical sciences, arts, and current events while refining reading and writing skills and developing thinking abilities.

The basic *Success* assumption means, in essence, that anything in print within reason—newspaper, textbook, novel, pamphlet, contract, magazine, letter, etc.—is a part of the reading curriculum materials. In the upper elementary grades, study topics are no longer inhibited by the predetermined chapter topics in textbooks, the various ancillary materials in a classroom, or the private collection of printed information gathered by an individual teacher.

Traditionally, the upper elementary schedule was established in segmented blocks—science, English, social studies, mathematics—mini-lessons within the academic day. The focus in that direction was not unwarranted, as teachers were urged to "teach reading in the content areas," although just how to accomplish this was never clearly shown. Somehow over the past three decades, reading too, became compartmentalized. Teachers were expected to plan specific and different lessons for each of the major content areas in addition to planning rather isolated reading lessons. In many instances, these "reading" lessons meant taking the basal readers from the desks or shelves and going through the motions of having students "read." Other "reading lessons" involved assigning a reading workbook page or copies of clearly labeled ditto master copies, usually according to reading skills. In numerous instances, students were assigned reading chores that had little to do with reading.

There was less and less time for students to read the hundreds of library books available to them, both fiction and content area-associated nonfiction. In thousands of classes, upper elementary students never saw or had an opportunity to read the daily newspaper. To make matters worse, many of these students did not have an opportunity to read the newspaper at home, either.

The transfer of reading ability from the reading activities of reading books and ancillary reading materials to the content area printed materials was not automatic. Publishers of some of the content area textbooks tried to alleviate the situation by "watering down" the printed content. This did not solve the problem and once again students were being deprived of opportunities to increase their communication skills as well as their conceptual development.

An analysis of the situation reveals the need to break the barriers that segregate instruction and introduce into the curriculum an eclectic approach that provides opportunities for the integration of the various aspects of instruction. For example, instructional time is better spent when students are finding verbs in a current events article in a newspaper than when students are given an isolated lesson on verbs that relates to nothing else. Some students apparently believe that they should study only science when it is time for the science lesson, usually involving the science textbooks or other educational materials specifically identified as science. Science information can be found in a variety of printed materials including fiction books, newspapers, and catalogues.

By accepting the idea that anything in print within reason is a part of reading curriculum materials and by eliminating predetermined vocabulary and content area topics, the *Success* program opens the doors for learning and teaching.

The teacher's knowledge and expertise are regarded highly in the *Success* program. Because of its openness, class instruction becomes a cooperative development with both student and teacher expanding module kernels. This concept, however, can be misused, if there is no base plan for the implementation of instruction. Students and teachers need some relevant and clearly identified perimeters within which they can build. This is how the modules become an asset to both teachers and students. It is paramount that you give specific directions in each module and follow through in giving assistance, so all students achieve *some* degree of success in following those directions before the end of each module.

Each module in the lessons found in Appendix One contains a suggested core teaching idea. You should develop these within the concept of the module, *according to your opinion of the best way to teach the module*, depending on the students in your class. For example, one teacher may wish to change a composition theme and a proofreading thrust. The suggestions in Appendix One serve as a springboard for teachers' ideas and for implementation of instruction. You should also present the module in the manner you find most comfortable. In all probability, no two classes will be alike; yet, all will have a base structure that integrates language arts instruction.

For years, educators have promoted individualization of instruction for students. It is time to openly promote individualization of teachers' methodologies and expertise. No two teachers will begin or develop any *Success* lesson in the same way. No two will use the same words, ask the same questions, or make the same points. If the concept of professionalism is endorsed, this is the way it should be. Many teachers of the *Success* program resent programs that suggest the lead-in avenues, even words they should say to students. After all, teachers are among the most highly educated people in the country. They should not be treated as if they had to be hand-held.

OBJECTIVES

The *Success* objectives are founded on the belief that not only can people learn through reading and writing, but that they can also integrate various facets of knowledge to gain new insights. *There is no educationally sound reason for a person to spend time learning to find a main idea within a paragraph unless the exercise contributes to that person's knowledge.* Students have told the authors one reason they don't like some reading classes is they don't get to read; they just "do" things. To get reading instruction into perspective, the overall objective is to provide opportunities for students to read a host of printed materials and to relate what they read to their own experiences. When reading skills improvement is *built into* this overall objective rather than towering over it, students not only read much more but they also improve their reading skills.

The following objectives of the *Success* program are practical and use common sense to promote the scholarly pursuit of knowledge:

1. Each student will have the opportunity to read a minimum of 500 library books during the academic year.
2. Each student will read the newspaper each school day.
3. Each student will read a variety of magazines, especially news and specialized magazines.
4. Each student will become increasingly aware of printed information related to various businesses and agencies.
5. Each student will improve reading skills *while* engaging in reading materials from a variety of academic or content areas.
6. Each student will learn about a variety of knowledge areas *while* experiencing extensive readings in both fiction and nonfiction.
7. Each student will write both factually and creatively each day, and include in some of the writings information read that day.
8. Each student will proofread his or her writing each day.
9. Each student will be asked to explain orally to the teacher and/or to another student the reason(s) for interpreting information read or written by that student.
10. Each student will learn to spell new words daily and will be tested on those words daily.
11. Each student will receive a balanced reading/ writing program including functional or survival reading, academic reading, recreational reading, and current events reading.
12. Each student will improve study skills in areas such as mathematics, social sciences, physical sciences, and humanities.

The basic assumption and objectives of the *Success* program combined with teacher expertise eliminate the concept that there is such a thing as a "fourth-grade book" or a topic of study exclusively reserved for students at a certain age. Instead, we promote the concept of students having opportunities to read and write about a variety of topics from a variety of printed materials and of teachers having opportunities to use their expertise to teach.

THE SUCCESS LESSONS

Each daily *Success* lesson lasts for two hours within the academic day, and is composed of four modules, each lasting approximately thirty minutes. Each module contains a different, yet complementary approach to teaching reading/writing.

The lessons are found in Appendix One of this book. You should start the program by teaching Lesson 1 either the first day of an academic year, or the day after reading this book during the year.

Each of the 12 specific objectives should be realized, in part, in each of the 180 lessons in the *Success* program. (There are usually 180 days in an academic year, and there are 180 lessons in this program.)

SCHEDULING THE FOUR MODULES WITHIN EACH LESSON

One *Success* lesson is taught each day after the program is started. As stated earlier, each lesson has four parts, or modules. Schedule a time to teach each of the four modules of the lesson.

The following are the four modules in a lesson with a hypothetical time schedule for each:

Phonics/Spelling Module	8:45 – 9:15
Composition Module	10:00 –10:30
Study Skills Module	1:00 – 1:30
Recreational Reading Module	2:15 – 2:45

An alternative schedule provides an uninterrupted time block for the modules, such as:

Phonics/Spelling Module	9:30–10:00
Composition Module	10:00–10:30
Study Skills Module	10:30–11:00
Recreational Reading Module	11:00–11:30

When you determine the time for each module, post the schedule containing both the name of each module and the times taught outside the classroom door. Posting the schedule will enable visitors to observe the teaching of specific modules at designated times. The procedure is also excellent in helping students learn to budget their time. Once it is posted, you should adhere as closely as possible to the module schedule each day, although it may be impossible to stay exactly on the 30-minute target. Especially at the beginning of the year, students may need more than 30 minutes for a module, with the exception of the Recreational Reading Module, until they learn the format and procedure of some of the internal assignments within the modules. Thirty minutes may be too long

at the beginning of the year for some students to read library books silently during the Recreational Reading Module. You may wish to start with 15 minutes for this module and gradually build to no more than 30 minutes.

Over a period of time students will develop a sixth sense for budgeting their time, and a sense of pride in their accomplishments. Every student will not complete all module work; however, the expectation is that every student will complete *some* of the work. If you allow additional time each day, such as an hour for a module, students who do not know how to budget their study time will be encouraged, subtly, to expect large blocks of additional time.

The remainder of the academic day is scheduled according to your individual preference or school policy for subjects such as mathematics, science, and art. Within the *Success* lesson, however, especially the Study Skills Module, there are specific content area lessons. Most teachers who teach the *Success* program incorporate daily content areas into the Study Skills Module. This provides a language arts correlation with content area topics, and still provides time for more in-depth study of the content area during other times in the school day. In other words, flexibility is built into the *Success* program so you can either follow the suggested topic in the *Success* lesson or substitute the topic with one that you plan to teach in a content area lesson that day.

CORRELATION OF THE MODULES

The balance within the four modules is designed to reinforce rather than to separate instruction. In each of the four modules within each *Success* lesson, students are encouraged to investigate for themselves printed information in an in-depth, rather than superficial, manner. The program rejects reading lessons where the focus is given to "improving" a reading skill (such as *locating supporting details*) in isolation from gaining knowledge. When refinement of reading and writing skills was made subservient to expanding knowledge areas (using topics such as *stratosphere*), we discovered not only that the reading/writing abilities of the students improved, but also that their knowledge was increased, and their motivation to read and write was higher

To ensure a balance in instruction, one aspect of language arts instruction that is strongly emphasized in one module is emphasized less in another module.

For example, in the Phonics/Spelling Module, emphasis is on spelling and grammatical usage of words associated with a given topic; whereas, in the Composition Module, emphasis is on fluency and content of written expression about the topic; however, improvement in correctness of writing is not ignored. Each day, each lesson adds new dimensions and also offers a review.

Remedial and enrichment components are woven into the lessons, rather than being separated from the major instructional focus. For example, an item introduced early in the year will be repeated several times during the year as *reviews*; however, the content and materials used for the item will be different. The academically talented student can learn new concepts and pursue previously learned concepts in greater depth. Academically talented students are not penalized while developmentally delayed students are achieving some success. This correlated reinforcement is essential to the success of the program.

In all fairness to you, to the program, and especially to the students, all four modules should be taught each day. Chapters Two through Five explain how to teach each module. When modules are omitted or repeated, a segment of the program is lost to the students. The program is designed to help you move students forward each day.

MAJOR PHASES IN THE PROGRAM

There are five major phases during the academic year. The phases are designed to reinforce each other and to add dimensions and new directions as the year progresses. There is also considerable overlap within the phases; the major difference in the phases is a matter of emphasis.

The phases are designed as follows:

TABLE 1-1

Phase	Lessons	Learning Theory Emphasis
1	1–10	Introductory
2	11–40	Transition
3	41–100	General
4	101–120	Reading/Writing Skill Associated with Knowledge
5	121–180	Diversity of Knowledge Areas

Phase 1—The Introductory Phase

Students are "getting started" in becoming able to perform the various processes within the modules, such as the daily spelling test, proofreading, and silent reading during the Recreational Reading Module. During this phase, all components of each module may not be completed because time must be allowed for ample explanations. As the students learn, for example, how to take the spelling test, more time will be available to complete the content suggestions in the modules. This is one way Phase 1 differs from the other phases.

Phase 1 introduces students to knowledge topics that are both concrete and abstract (*circus/education*) coupled with reading and writing skills. The skills begin to improve as the students' knowledge about the topic increases. The basic *Success* concept in each module, except the Recreational Reading Module, is that by talking, reading, writing, thinking, and defending their ideas with facts and interpretations, the students' learning will take on new meaning.

Phase 2—The Transition Phase

This phase starts for most students on the eleventh day of instruction and is emphasized through Lesson 40. Each day, students should become more proficient in the learning strategies, such as proofreading and volunteering words with a certain spelling cluster. The kinds of knowledge areas and skills introduced during the Transition Phase are the foundation for success in later phases. A comparison of papers written in Lesson 2 of the Introductory Phase with papers written in Lesson 39 of the Transition Phase should reveal tangible evidence of student progress. There are, therefore, different and distinct teaching techniques used in Phase 2 that are not used in other phases.

Phase 3—The General Phase

The third phase continues through Lesson 100, and emphasizes the first level of expanding knowledge while improving reading and writing skills. The strategies for learning how to complete the module assignments have been learned, and the students can concentrate on getting the work completed and feeling good about it. You will only have to teach the strategies, such as the spelling test format, to any new students who may enter the class. During Phase 3 there is a definite aspect of expanding content not possible in the first two phases.

Phase 4—The Reading/Writing Skills Associated with Knowledge Areas Phase

This is the phase that encourages students to use skills taught in previous phases as interpretive tools in their applied expansion of knowledge. Such an emphasis on skills in earlier phases is not advisable. For example, during Phase 4, the writing of factual reports enables the student to demonstrate research skills that have been introduced earlier in the Study Skills Module. Each lesson combines a knowledge topic from science, social studies, mathematics, art, and other content areas with a reading and writing assignment. The student reads a model containing information about the knowledge area and then writes his or her version of the model, incorporating in the writing what has been learned.

If, for example, a local controversy is the topic of a newspaper editorial, students discuss the controversy, read the editorial, and explain their position by writing an editorial. This exercise demonstrates *applied expansion of knowledge*. To integrate a segment focus, the module will specify a reading/writing skill, such as the inclusion of a *prepositional phrase containing adjectives* for the student to incorporate in the writing and to detect if there is a prepositional phrase with an adjective in the printed editorial.

An additional example of the emphasis in this phase in which students use a textbook is as follows: Students read three paragraphs in a social studies textbook assigned by the teacher. The assignment can be associated with a topic being studied in a social studies unit already under way. The students write their interpretation of the major information in those paragraphs, including any additional information that is related to the topic. Their writing is in three paragraphs in the mode found in the social studies textbook. In addition, they include one *comparison*, which is the segment focus, in the writing and reread the text to see if a comparison is found in the three paragraphs. The use of the reading model prior to student writing is paramount in this phase, but should not be emphasized prior to Phase 4.

Phase 5—The Diversity of Knowledge Areas Phase

This phase is emphasized during Lessons 121–180. Each day a different knowledge area is suggested about which to discuss, read, and write. The study skill changes daily, and, coupled with the daily changing of knowledge areas, students acquire a vast amount of new information, while steadily improving their reading and writing skills. Some of the knowledge areas are academic, such as the study of bacteria, while other areas, such as how to install a CB radio in an automobile, are not considered traditional academic topics.

DAILY OPENING ACTIVITY

The first activity each morning after items such as announcements should be the following:

1. Open that day's newspaper to one section (front page, society, stock market, classified advertisements) and comment about something in the section. The teacher should not read an entire article to the class. Ask students who are interested in learning more about the topic discussed to read about it in the newspaper at some time during the day.

2. Read selected information from a different section of the newspaper each day, thus introducing students to the various parts of a newspaper. Information of particular interest discussed the previous day(s) should receive brief comments concerning the most recent developments.

3. From a vocabulary development standpoint, select one key word or phrase from a headline and discuss its meaning with reference to the article's focus. In sections of the newspaper such as classified advertisements that have no headlines, discuss a key word or phrase within one segment.

THE FIRST WEEKS OF SCHOOL

Most teachers who have taught the *Success* program indicate it takes approximately three weeks for their students to become familiar with the procedure within each module. For example, a spelling test is given each day as the last part of the Phonics/Spelling Module. During the first weeks, teach students to move into the test as a part of this module; thereafter, students take the test without procedural instruction from you.

Do not expect a smooth beginning in any module; however, do not become discouraged and discontinue any modules. The module formats are designed to encourage student independence in completing work, even if the work only consists of a few words at the beginning of the year.

Because time is needed to teach students how to complete the modules, the content of the first two–three weeks within each module is reduced. Note the items added to increase content as less time is needed for procedural instruction. For example, compare the content of Lesson 1 with Lesson 30.

THE MATERIALS

The materials in the *Success* program should be varied in both reading difficulty and content. The objective is to teach students to read any material they encounter and may need or want to read.

Among the materials needed to teach this program are:

one copy of *Success in Reading and Writing: Grade Four* for the teacher

one copy of *Success in Reading and Writing: Grade Four* for the principal

one copy of *Success in Reading and Writing: Grade Four* for any parents who wish to supplement the lessons through discussions at home

one adult-type dictionary for each student

mathematics, science, social studies, health, and music textbooks from different publishers, grade levels two through eight

chart paper and magic markers

three manila folders per student

three cardboard boxes to hold the folders containing students' writings from three of the modules

paper for students to write on

one spiral notebook per student for use in the Phonics/Spelling Module

one spiral notebook per student for use in the Study Skills Module

classroom subscriptions to at least five copies of a local newspaper per academic day, Monday–Friday

classroom subscriptions to at least five magazines, September–June (*Newsweek* and *Time* are especially recommended)

encyclopedias (one set per classroom if possible)

several thesauruses

maps, catalogues, telephone books, various forms, and other survival reading materials such as coupons

Arrangements should be made with the school librarian to check out in the name of the class a minimum of 50 library books every three weeks

These books are in addition to the books checked out individually by students.

Workbook pages, printed segments from "kits," and such should not be used during the two-hour lesson, although they might be incorporated at other times during the day. The *Success* concept includes students learning to *apply* skills to any relevant materials, instead of their spending learning time filling in blanks, etc. on materials that are artificial and not pertinent.

Do not wait until all materials are on a budget line to start the *Success* program. The teachers of some of the *Success* classes asked friends, parents of students in their classes, and others to donate newspapers, magazines, telephone books, maps, encyclopedias, etc. and the teachers brought these items to school for use in their class. This is not ideal; however, until such time as school budgets provide these items, teachers may need to spearhead the movement by advising the administration of the need for such materials.

GROUPING

In the *Success* program, each module is introduced to the entire class. You then simply move from student to student helping each achieve some success in whatever task that student is attempting. Trying to identify artificial "reading levels" is of little importance. What is important is if a student gets meaning from news articles, books, etc., and has developed the desire to want to try to read and write anything within reason. When the small group stereotyping is eliminated, there is greater opportunity for students to help each other, no matter what the printed material contains. *Greater individualization of instruction occurs when grouping is eliminated.*

Trying to teach students in three to six groups is eliminated in the *Success* program. The planning time is a tremendous drain on the teacher, and chances are, as long as some students are placed in groups where the expectations are low, they will continue to be underachievers. It is also extremely doubtful that anyone likes to be branded as "behind the others" for nine months each year—no matter how subtle the maneuver.

CORRELATION OF READING WITH WRITING INSTRUCTION

Reading and writing lessons are merged to reinforce each other in producing successful learning experiences instead of giving reading assignments that do not relate to writing lessons and vice versa. There are several benefits to this organizational arrangement. First, what the student writes in response to a reading assignment can serve as an obvious check of his or her reading comprehension. Second, writing gives students a new perspective on reading and the factors with which an author must be concerned. This has a significantly positive effect on reading comprehension. When students can clearly express a thought in writing with evidence supporting that thought, they learn more about main idea, supporting details, cause and effect, proper sequence, and other comprehension skills than numerous multiple-choice exercises could teach. Further, the many writing exercises give students opportunities to think through and express ideas for someone else to read. Finally, just as nothing improves reading more effectively than more reading, practice is the greatest teacher of writing. The variety of reading and writing activities provide students with many avenues to continually develop a sense of personal pride in achievement in both reading and writing.

VOCABULARY SELECTION

Two kinds of vocabulary are the backbones of this program. The words from students in the class constitute a major part of the vocabulary studied. Vocabulary in various kinds of printed materials read and studied by the students is the other source.

There is no controlled vocabulary, no isolated list of sight words, no staged sequence of stories to be read. No one predetermines that some words are "too difficult" for some people, a practice used in the past with lists of words graded according to "difficulty level." The *Success* program is designed to continue basic word analysis skills so students can attempt to decode *any word* they need to read.

READING COMPREHENSION

Checks of comprehension should be made on an individual, spontaneous basis and not in a predeter-

mined fashion. For example, you might ask one student, "What does this mean to *you*?" as he or she reads a newspaper headline; ask the next student to relate one instance in a sports story, and another, "What was the name of the winning team?" From the individual student's oral and/or written responses should come the next comprehension questions. Although it would be nice to prepackage this information, comprehension checks should be highly individualized and in reality cannot be planned in advance. Word meanings should be included in phrase, sentence, paragraph, or chapter context, rather than in fragmented, isolated settings.

REVIEW

A pattern of crisscross reviews is *built into* the internal aspects of the *Success* program rather than placed as entities separated from the mainstream of instruction. As just one example, during the Recreational Reading Module, there is a review item from either the Phonics/Spelling or Composition Modules. The teacher notes the review element and uses it only with students who need the extra help, also allowing for highly individualized instruction.

HOMEWORK

Homework is another basic feature of the *Success* program. Each student should take at least one book home as often as school policy allows; we hope this can be every school night. Occasionally, ask a student to tell another something he or she read the previous night.

In addition, a daily homework assignment is given as a part of most Phonics/Spelling Modules and in some of the Composition and Study Skills Modules. You can also assign appropriate pages from content area textbooks to supplement module topics.

VISITORS, VOLUNTEERS, AND AIDES

The classes should be open to the public during the two-hour lesson after the first 40 days of instruction. It will take at least 40 days to have a quantity of student writings in the files and a variety of charts displayed in the classroom. Since there is an ongoing sense of direction and balance in teaching reading and writing, visitors and volunteers have been welcomed by teachers who have taught the *Success* program. Teachers simply ask the visitor to sit beside a student and help him or her complete the module under way. Likewise, there was no need for the teacher to be burdened with making additional plans for aides or volunteers that did not conform to the lesson taking place.

Educational jargon to explain the program is unnecessary since its directness is almost self-explanatory. The lesson plans in Appendix One are open on your desk; you have developed each module according to your expertise and best judgment; the students know what is expected; and folders contain a partial record of student progress thus far in the academic year. It is immediately apparent to the visitor, volunteer, or aide that positive things are happening.

ACCOUNTABILITY: WRITTEN RECORDS OF STUDENTS' WORK

The record-keeping emphasis in this program is on student performance, evidence of progress, and positive self-concept because they realize they are achieving. Teachers are *not* taking valuable time checking skill boxes or making numerical or letter notations during the two-hour lessons. The *Success* modules speak for themselves and are extremely impressive when viewed over a period of months.

Each student should write a paper each day in the first three modules. The students place their writing in a folder with their name and file it in a cardboard box labeled with the name of the module. As soon as possible, each student should *file his or her own paper* in the appropriate box. If you use only one box, it may get too full. You may wish to have two or three boxes labeled *Composition*, for example, and divide the class folders alphabetically in halves or thirds.

Students' work can also be kept in individual composition books. Each student should have a separate notebook for each of the first three modules. These notebooks should be kept in a central place, should be used only during the appropriate module, and should not be taken home until the end of the year. When a notebook is filled, it should be filed away and another one begun. More specific directions on how to use the students' folders or notebooks as a longitudinal record of progress are found in the following chapters.

Have students date each paper and *don't send them home until the end of the academic year*. These folders provide a longitudinal record of each student's work. The folders become quite thick in size and are extremely helpful in parent-teacher conferences. Papers completed by students during other parts of the day may or may not be sent home, depending on your judgment.

Students should correct their own errors on these papers. As noted earlier, you should move from student to student making comments about their work. When you spot an error, call it to the student's attention; however, the *student does the correcting*. In addition, a student may spot a spelling error made in October and correct the error in January as proofreading skills improve.

Chapter Five describes how to keep records of books read by students. The student folders and the record of books read provide more information about each student's reading/writing abilities and disabilities than any standardized or criterion referenced test score can ever indicate.

STUDENTS WITH SEVERE READING DISABILITIES

Even though students with severe reading disabilities cannot achieve success in every part of every module, they should not be segregated from their classmates. The nonreaders and nonwriters receive the same directions as their peers; however, during each module, when you work individually with students at their desks, these students should receive special instruction. In essence, you adjust that assignment to afford flexibility and individualization of instruction. For example, you could place your hand over the hand of a nonwriter and guide that student in the formation of the letter(s) being studied in the Phonics/Spelling Module. The object for this student is to learn to write a letter or even a part of that letter, and the student should be praised for efforts and achievements. For these students, achievement is comparable to that of writers accomplishing more advanced work—it is all a matter of perspective.

As you work with a disabled reader at his or her desk, help the student locate, decode and comprehend words. For example, the teacher, without singling out a particular student by putting that student in a "group," moves to a reading disabled student working at his or her desk and—

helps the student locate a word or phrase associated

with the focus of the module being studied

helps the student pronounce the word

helps the student read the sentence containing the word

discusses the meaning of the word(s) according to use in the sentence

repeats the procedure using other words located by the student

These words might be in newspapers or textbooks, in library books or on another student's paper, depending on which materials and which module is underway. Again, the student should receive positive comments on attempts to read. Since the students are not removed from the introductory parts of each module, they observe the reading/writing process each day. This instruction, coupled with the teacher's individualization at their desks, will in time move these students from illiteracy.

SUCCESS IN REMEDIAL READING CLASSES

The *Success* program can be adapted for use in a reading laboratory or remedial reading classes. Modifications will usually be necessary due to time constraints. One possible schedule is suggested below:

Monday	Tuesday
Recreational Reading Module	Recreational Reading Module
Composition Module	Composition Module
Study Skills Module	Study Skills Module

Wednesday	Thursday
Phonics/Spelling Module	Recreational Reading Module
Composition Module	Phonics/Spelling Module
Study Skills Module	

Friday
Recreational Reading Module
Phonics/Spelling Module

Each module will take less than the regularly allotted time period with this schedule, since with a smaller number of students, thirty minutes will not be necessary for each module. Composition and Study Skills Modules should alternate every week. Different schedules could be established by varying the pattern as long as continuity within each module is preserved. Individual lessons will sometimes have to be modified to meet specific needs and abilities of students.

THE TEACHER AS A PROFESSIONAL

In this program, you are accorded the status due an intelligent person with professional educational expertise. You are *not* charged with clerical chores, such as checking boxes on student skill sheets, parroting questions and other ideas from a "canned" teacher's guide, or any other robot-type set of activities.

The program is designed to demonstrate that (1) teachers can teach; (2) students can learn an amazing amount of information; (3) academic textbooks are only *one* type of reference material; and (4) reading and writing are keystones for both liberal and technical education. This program departs from traditional approaches because it widens the scope of knowledge areas and does not restrict youngsters to particular lessons. Just as the *Success* program recognizes the intelligence and expertise of teachers, it encourages students' thinking powers as they encounter a myriad of basic and creative learning areas.

The *Success* program is a reorganization of the language arts curriculum. Prior to implementing the lessons in this program, you should study the rationale, the chapters containing information on how to teach the modules, then the lessons containing the modules. Note how the various modules reinforce each other, the built-in reviews as opposed to isolated reviews, the techniques to expand knowledge rather than limit exposure to various topics, and the approaches to research by students.

The *Success* program affords a base structure that is flexible. In all probability, each teacher will teach each of the 720 modules in a different way, according to that teacher's experience and instructional techniques; however, the core of each module remains the same—the correlation of reading, writing, spelling, thinking, speaking, defending one's work orally, and filing papers. An eclectic approach that correlates a selection of specific knowledge areas and skills seems to be one of the keys to success in learning. The person responsible for turning the key is you, the teacher. In the *Success* program, you are viewed as a professional educator, rather than as a technician.

COMMUNICATING WITH PARENTS

It is important that school personnel and parents know about the *Success* program; therefore, communication about the program and invitations to encourage visitors to observe the modules being taught is advisable.

You and/or your students can send weekly newsletters home to parents giving examples of acitivities that have been completed in the classroom. Suggestions to parents on how they can reinforce classroom activities can be included, also. The following is an example of such a newsletter:

NEWSLETTER TO PARENTS FROM ROOM 14

This week we have concentrated on words containing the spelling clusters *br, cl, fr, dr,* and *gr.* Ask your child to give you words containing these clusters or to locate words containing these clusters for items in your home.

Writing comparisons and locating different parts of speech has also kept us busy during the week. You can give your child practice with comparisons by encouraging him or her to compare items found in your home.

Our class won the soccer game this week and that makes us the "champs."

Some teachers who have taught the *Success* program have held a Parents' Night at the school. The teachers demonstrate each module and encourage parents to look through the folders containing their child's work.

During parent-teacher conferences, you need to explain the *Success* program to parents, and provide time for them to look through the longitudinal records of their child's work.

Parents can also be involved in an evaluation of the *Success* program. One teacher, for example, near the end of the year gave parents an opportunity to make written comments about the program. Comments such as the following were returned to school:

"My child's reading has really improved. Signing his papers gives us a chance to see what he is doing."

"My child likes reading and spelling for us because she likes to show off what she has learned and it makes us proud of her."

"My involvement in her homework is good. Having to sign her homework is a good way to make sure she does it right."

ADMINISTRATORS

Administrators need to be knowledgeable of the *Success* program. Following are some ways administrators can aid teachers in implementing the program:

1. Provide the necessary materials.
2. Communicate support to teachers and parents.
3. Afford time for teachers to meet with other teachers in their school and/or other schools to share ideas.
4. Visit classrooms regularly and get involved in helping students during the modules.

When visiting a *Success* class, an administrator should look for the following:

1. Charts displayed in the classroom.
2. Students' longitudinal folders.
3. A wide range of materials visible in the classroom.
4. Each student achieving some degree of success in each module.
5. No ability grouping.
6. The lesson and module being taught as found in the *Success in Reading and Writing: Grade Four* book on the teacher's desk.

chapter two
How to Teach the Phonics/Spelling Module

The Phonics/Spelling Module provides instruction in reading, writing, and spelling. Students also learn to make logical associations between the words they study and specific topics. This module is usually taught as the first 30-minute part of each *Success* lesson.

The Phonics/Spelling Modules are found in the first column of each lesson in Appendix One.

SPELLING

In the *Success* program, the spelling lessons are derived from words students volunteer during class discussions about a variety of subjects and from words that you assign. Discussions concern both academic and nonacademic topics and are developed according to the knowledge and interests of the students with your direction and support. Spelling words from these discussions becomes a lively, integral part of most of the Phonics/Spelling Modules.

A spelling program such as this differs from the traditional spelling program in several ways. Instead of lists of words to memorize that have no relationship to the other material studied during the day, spelling words in the *Success* program are an integral part of the reading lesson. They are words that the students have interest in and need to know how to spell. Instead of waiting until Friday, a spelling test is given

daily during the Phonics/Spelling Module. Procedure for the daily spelling test is described later under Step 3 in the section "Major Steps in Teaching the Module." Traditional spelling textbooks may be used as sources for supplemental assignments; however, they are not the core of spelling instruction.

PHONICS

Instruction in the relationship between symbols and the sounds they represent in words is directly related to other aspects of the reading program, just as spelling instruction is. This is essential in helping students transfer learning from their phonics lessons to their other reading assignments.

In the phonics part of the Phonics/Spelling Module, a different letter combination is emphasized each day during many of the modules. The combinations are not limited to primary level phonics emphases, such as consonant blends and digraphs, but are representative of the thousands of letter combinations found in words. Since the letters surrounding a particular letter within a word can alter its sound, *sounds* of letters in isolation are not taught. Instead, students learn the *spelling of words that contain a specified letter combination or cluster*. For example, the sound made by *ar* in *apartment* is different from the sound made by the same letter cluster in *around*.

Such an approach to sound-symbol relationships is flexible enough to take into account the differences in pronunciation due to the geographical location and dialect spoken by the students.

PHONICS/SPELLING MODULE COMPONENTS

Each daily Phonics/Spelling Module includes:

1. A *spelling emphasis*, such as *b*, *ance*, or *gn*, for students to identify within words.
2. A *vocabulary emphasis*, such as *plants*, *entertainment*, or *time*, as a topic for discussion and stimulus for associated words the students may generate.
3. The opportunity for *students to suggest words* that (a) include only the spelling emphasis, (b) relate only to the vocabulary emphasis, or (c) include both the spelling emphasis and relate to the vocabulary emphasis. In some Phonics/Spelling Modules, printed materials such as newspapers, textbooks, and magazines are suggested as reference material for students to locate printed information they can associate with the vocabulary emphasis and/or words containing the spelling emphasis.
4. A *chart of words* volunteered by the students which is displayed in the classroom for 15–20 days as a reference material for review, spelling assistance, and a record of the students' ideas.
5. A *list*, recorded by each student, of the words he or she selected to learn that day, and any additional information called for in the lesson.
6. A *spelling test* checked immediately by another student.
7. *Filing* by each student of his or her spelling test paper in a manila folder.
8. A *homework assignment* completed in the spiral notebook, signed by parents, and checked the next academic day by the teacher.
9. A quick *oral test* given by parents each night on the words selected by the student that day in school.

VOCABULARY/DISCUSSION CYCLES IN THE ACADEMIC YEAR

The Phonics/Spelling Module contains a tremendous variety of topics. The *content emphasis* within the module changes during the year, depending on the *cycle* stressed. Each cycle has a different focus.

Table 2-1 is a list of the cycles in the Phonics/Spelling Module, the lessons included in each cycle, and the emphasis for each cycle. Additional details about the cycle are found later in this chapter.

TABLE 2–1

PHONICS/SPELLING CYCLES		
Cycle	Lessons	Cycle Emphasis
1—Part 1	1–10	Introductory Discussions
1—Part 2	11–60	Current Events Vocabulary with Spelling Emphases
2	61–90	Academic Vocabulary with Structural Emphasis
3	91–110	Linguistic/Structural Emphasis Study
4	111–125	Function Words with Spelling Emphasis
5	126–140	Recreation Words with Structural Emphasis
6	141–180	Expanding Vocabulary with Spelling Emphasis

Within each module, reading, writing, spelling, listening, and speaking are correlated. To expedite learning in any cycle during the year, a basic four-step format is suggested for teaching each Phonics/Spelling Module.

MAJOR STEPS IN TEACHING THE PHONICS/SPELLING MODULE

The basic structure of the module contains four steps. Although each of these steps should be included daily, the *Success* program provides for the differences in individual teaching styles, knowledge, and expertise, by encouraging variations in the way the steps of the lessons are developed. Possible variations are suggested in the following description of each step. In this way, individual differences among teachers is recognized, but the students are taught according to a logical, educationally sound, developmental plan.

At the beginning of the year, it is important for students to learn the steps involved in the Phonics/Spelling Module and to be able to move from one step to the next smoothly during the 30–40 minutes allotted for each module.

The four steps, in sequential order, used in teaching each Phonics/Spelling Module are:

Step 1: The Development of the Vocabulary Chart
Step 2: Students' Word Lists and Other Writing
Step 3: The Daily Spelling Test
Step 4: The Homework Assignment

Each step is explained later in this chapter, and is accompanied by examples of teacher-made charts and student work.

Step 1: The Development of the Spelling Charts

This step should take approximately 10–12 minutes of the 30-minute module.

Lessons 1–10: Introductory Discussions—Vocabulary Area Only. Write the vocabulary emphasis at the top of a sheet of chart paper; the chart paper is usually attached to the chalkboard with masking tape. Suggested vocabulary topics are found in each Phonics/Spelling Module in Appendix One.

The students volunteer words, phrases, or sentences they can associate with the vocabulary emphasis. As they volunteer the words, write them on the chart. At times there may be discussion of the meaning of the words; other times it will not be necessary to discuss the words.

Figure 2–1 is a chart developed in a fourth-grade class during the Phonics/Spelling Module, Lesson 4, and shows the basic chart format during Part 1 of Cycle 1.

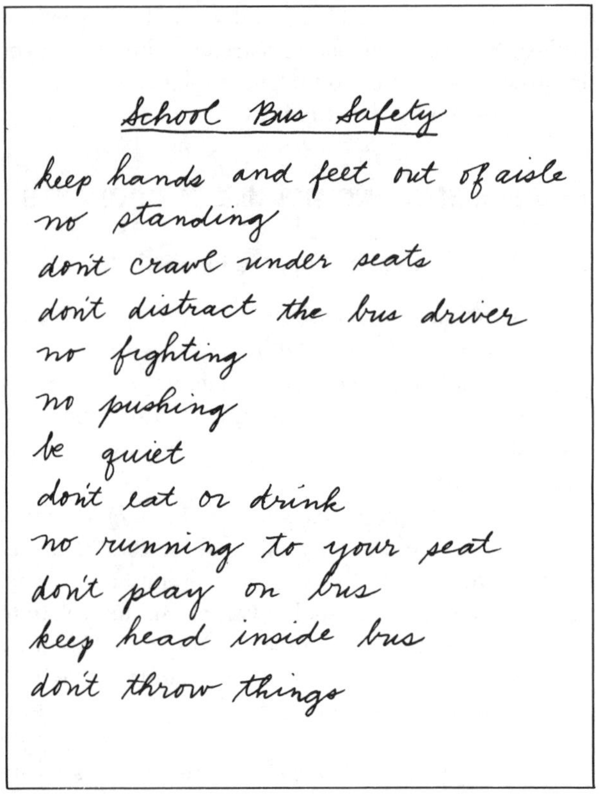

Lessons 11–180: Addition of Spelling or Structural Emphasis to Vocabulary Emphasis. During the first ten lessons, students volunteer only words they associate with a certain discussion or vocabulary focus. Beginning with Lesson 11, students read in a *newspaper, magazine, textbook*, or other printed material to find words they can associate with a vocabulary emphasis (e.g., *people*), or that contains a spelling emphasis (e.g., *tr*), or that contains a structural emphasis (e.g., prefix *un*). Students may volunteer words that contain the spelling or structural emphasis, but that cannot be associated with the vocabulary emphasis. Likewise, they may give words that relate

FIGURE 2–1   Phonics/Spelling Class Chart from Lesson 4

to the vocabulary emphasis but do not contain the spelling or structural emphasis. In this way, students learn to correlate their vocabulary and knowledge with spelling.

Beginning with Lesson 11, write both the spelling emphasis, structural emphasis, and/or discussion focus at the top of the chart before asking students to volunteer words.

Figures 2–2 and 2–3 illustrate two different ways you can structure the charts once the vocabulary and spelling or structural emphasis are added after Lesson 10. In Figure 2–2, the teacher recorded words containing the *sp* spelling as volunteered by students using *newspapers*. This chart does not contain words associated with the vocabulary emphasis, which is *entertainment* in this particular module. The association of the words to the concept of *entertainment* was made orally in class by teacher and students.

Figure 2–3 has two sections. At the top of the chart the teacher recorded words containing the *wh* spelling volunteered by students from *newspaper* reading. Only words with two or three syllables were

14

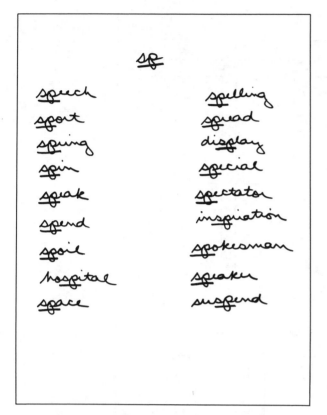

FIGURE 2–2 Phonics/Spelling Class Chart from Lesson 19—Spelling and Vocabulary Emphasis

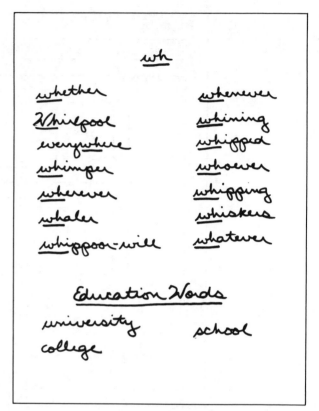

FIGURE 2–3 Phonics/Spelling Class Chart from Lesson 31, Adaptation of Chart— Spelling and Vocabulary Emphasis

recorded at the *top* of the chart. At the *bottom* of the chart, the teacher wrote words found by the students in newspapers that relate directly to the vocabulary emphasis, which is *education* in this particular module in Lesson 31.

When a word contained both the spelling emphasis and was related also to the vocabulary emphasis, the class decided on which area of the chart from Lesson 31 the teacher should place the word. Individual teachers should develop the chart using the format they prefer.

When a student volunteers a word or cluster of words that contain the spelling or structural emphasis and/or is related to the discussion topic, write the word(s) on the chart. If a word is volunteered, yet the student cannot associate it with the topic and it does not contain the spelling or structural elements emphasized in the module, write the word on the chalkboard, not on the chart paper, and briefly discuss the word. In either case, write down the student's word.

When the whole class participates in locating the words at the beginning of each Phonics/Spelling Mod-

ule, there rarely is difficulty in getting a sufficient number of words to develop a chart. If there should be long periods between students volunteering words, however, you should give a word containing either the spelling or structural emphasis or related to the vocabulary topic, or ask students to suggest suitable words not found in print. It is important to keep the module moving at a constant pace.

The development of a class vocabulary chart is an essential part of the Phonics/Spelling Module *each day*. The chart contains words volunteered by the students. Although you can and should provide words for the chart, the majority of the words should be volunteered by students. These charts are *not* the traditional word lists prepared by teachers prior to a class.

There are several instructional purposes for the charts. Initially, students have to locate words in print that are appropriate for that day's chart. They improve their skimming and scanning skills as well as learning to think of associations between their words and an assigned topic. They observe the process as you write

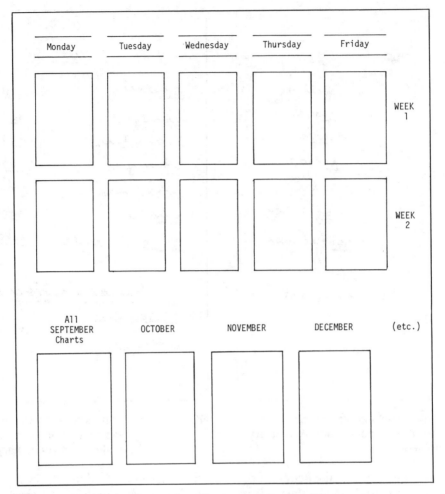

Monday	Tuesday	Wednesday	Thursday	Friday	
					WEEK 1
					WEEK 2

All SEPTEMBER Charts	OCTOBER	NOVEMBER	DECEMBER	(etc.)

FIGURE 2–4   One Method to Display Phonics/Spelling Charts

and others read their words. Further, since the charts are displayed in the classroom for at least 15–20 days, the students can refer to the words for help in spelling, discussion ideas, and thinking of words containing certain spelling combinations or structural aspects for new charts.

Figure 2–4 shows one way charts can be displayed in a classroom. Some teachers elect to display each chart for two or three months on bulletin boards or hang them by clothespins on lines strung across the classroom.

Optional Chart Review Test

In the Phonics/Spelling Modules in Appendix One, a Chart Review Test is suggested every *tenth* day. This is optional. You may select words from the latest ten charts and construct a review test, or you

may ask the students to create their own review test using words from the charts. If the students decide to select their own words for the review test, you may wish to identify certain important words as "Teacher's Words" which are mandatory for all students to study for the spelling review test. The "Teacher's Words" would appropriately be those associated with a unit being taught during a different part of the school day.

The "Teacher's Words" concept can also be used daily for the spelling test. For example, you might identify a few key words for all students to study and to spell during the daily test.

No two teachers teach the Phonics/Spelling Modules exactly alike. Different lead-ins, examples, and discussions can be used. No two classes volunteer identically the same words; therefore, no two classrooms will have the same charts displayed. Yet, all teachers should begin the Phonics/Spelling Modules with the basic structure of suggested elements and develop a class chart containing words volunteered by the students.

Step 2: Students' Word List and Other Writings

This step should take approximately 10–12 minutes, and follows the development of the vocabulary chart.

In the second part of the Phonics/Spelling Module, students incorporate the earlier reading, spelling, speaking, and listening aspects in the module with *writing*. You may use different approaches to teaching this part of the module. The following are two major variations of the basic structure for completing Step 2 of the Phonics/Spelling Module.

Variation 1. After the chart has been completed, each student selects words to learn to spell during the third 10–12 minutes (Step 3). The words can be selected from the chart; however, *the words must contain at least one of the elements suggested in the module for that day.*

Students copy their words on a page in a spiral-bound notebook that they have dated and that should not be removed from the notebook. When the notebook is filled, the teacher files the notebook and the student begins a new one. The notebooks are extremely helpful in teacher-parent conferences and in the student's own review of his or her progress.

Students then write sentences or paragraphs, depending on the directions from the teacher, using some of the words selected for the spelling test (Step 3). These sentences or paragraphs usually deal with the topic discussed during the chart development part of the module.

Figure 2–5 is an example of a page from one student's notebook during Lesson 14 with the list of words the student selected from that day's chart, sentences written by the student in class before the spelling test, and the parent's signature for homework. This student took the spelling test on a sheet of loose-leaf notebook paper which was filed in a manila folder containing all spelling test papers of that student.

Variation 2. After the chart has been developed, you may elect to have students write their sentences or paragraphs and underline the words they wish to learn to spell. The students then copy the underlined words in a list below their writing so they will be ready for their spelling test.

Students volunteer words associated with famous *musicians*, for example, according to their understanding of the word "famous." They then could write sentences. Each student's sentences would be different from those written by other students. The student can indicate words he or she will try to learn to spell before the spelling test that day. Another student can then call out the words orally and count the number of points awarded for correct spelling responses. (See Step 3 of the Phonics/Spelling Module.)

Step 3: The Daily Spelling Test

This step should take 10–12 minutes.

Step 3 is an individual spelling test of some of the words included in the student's writing in Step 2, and from the chart developed in Step 1. Students choose words they have written and that they think they can quickly learn to spell. *You may add important words that all students should attempt to spell in addition to words selected by the students.* These might be words associated with a content area unit being studied during another part of the day or functional words, such as *poison, telephone,* or *danger.* Until students learn the *procedure* for taking the spelling test, they should select only *one* word.

Procedure. The students spend a few minutes in silent study of their chosen list. When ready to be tested, they locate a partner who is also ready to spell and exchange papers. Most teachers prefer to have daily tests given *orally* because it takes less time and it is not necessary to ask the student to write the words again during the module. The number of words spelled varies daily and depends on individual students.

It is important, however, that students speak slowly and enunciate each letter clearly. During the actual spelling test, the student who is spelling orally to another student should not face the charts until after the word(s) is spelled.

Scoring. As one student spells a word orally, the partner writes a small check mark *above each letter said in the proper sequence.* If the student misses any part of the word, no points are given; however, the student receives one point for each letter in words that are spelled correctly. (This procedure is different from the one used in the second and third grade *Success* program.)

As soon as students become aware that the longer the word, the more points received, most stu-

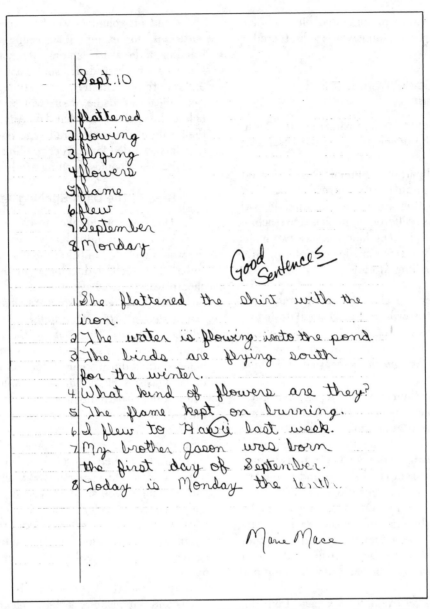

FIGURE 2–5   One Student's Phonics/Spelling Writing During Lesson 14—
Phonics/Spelling Writing: Variation 1

dents want to spell longer words. The following are examples of checks during the spelling test:

1. *gravity* (*gravity* spelled correctly) = 7 points
2. *spaice* (*space* spelled incorrectly) = 0 points
3. *astronaut* (*astronaut* spelled correctly) = 9 points

   Total points = 16

Variation 1.   Variation 1 is described above. As soon as the student has finished writing the words and thinks he or she can spell them, the student locates another student as a partner who has also finished writing and studying the spelling words. They exchange notebooks, give each other the spelling test *orally*, and mark one point for each letter in words spelled correctly; no points for misspelled words. Figure 2–6 is a sample of a student's writing.

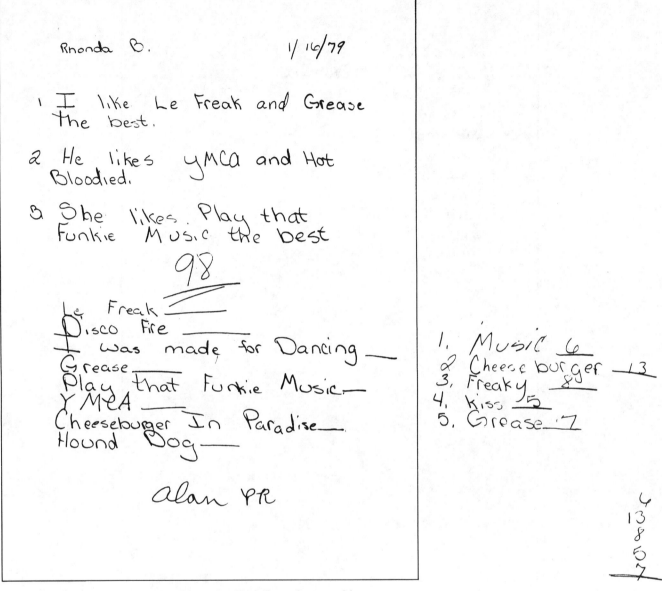

FIGURE 2–6   Example of a Student's Spelling Test—Lesson 81

Variation 2. Some teachers prefer a daily *written* test of the student's spelling list. It follows much the same procedure as the oral test, only the student writes the words on a sheet of paper, and dates and files this test in a manila folder that can be kept in the student's desk or in a box labeled *Phonics/Spelling Papers*. Figure 2–7 is an example of a written spelling test.

These daily spelling tests serve as important documentation that can be used for parent-teacher con-

ferences and as references for grading by the teacher. Teachers concerned about recording spelling grades can collect papers from time to time and check them rather than having partners check the tests.

Chart Review Test

Another option in the Phonics/Spelling Module is the *Chart Review Test*. This test is suggested in the

19

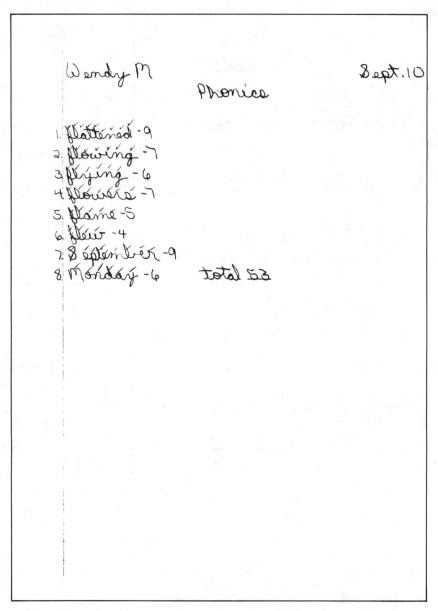

FIGURE 2–7   Example of a Student's Written Spelling Test—Variation 1 of Step 2

Phonics/Spelling Modules in Appendix One at ten-day intervals.

You may suggest a particular focus for the review test. Ask students to "select the most important words for the review," or "choose words you *did not* test on before." The lists may be individual, or you may wish to make a Review Test Chart with the help of the students for the whole class to study.

You, the students, or the whole class together, may decide on the number of words required for the Review Test. It is suggested that the number not be a set one, but might begin with 6–10 words and increase to 15–20 words or more as the year progresses.

After the list is decided upon, the students study silently for a few minutes and then test with a partner, or as a whole class writing activity.

The Review Tests may be checked and filed as usual, or you may decide to check and file them to determine students' progress. They can be used as a measurement tool for grades since the words have been on display for at least ten days, and the students have had exposure to these lists.

The Chart Review Test is to be considered *optional*, and should be used at your discretion. It is included in the *Success* program as a built-in review of the words being introduced to the students.

Step 4: Homework Assignments

This step may be presented orally at the end of the Phonics/Spelling Module, or you may write it on the chalkboard at any time during the module.

Specific homework assignments are suggested in many of the Phonics/Spelling Modules; however, you are encouraged to adapt or change these to fit the needs of your students. The homework assignments lend themselves to a variety of materials. Although the traditional spelling textbook can be incorporated in the homework assignments, the assignments can be given with reference to any printed material in homes.

Teaching students to keep their list of words in a notebook and to complete their homework assignment daily is an important aspect of the Phonics/Spelling Module. When the notebook is taken home each night, parents have an opportunity to be involved with their child's learning experiences. If they give a short oral test of that day's word list or only sign their name indicating they have checked their child's homework, parents are positively reinforcing their child's learning. They are also aware of what is taking place at school during a part of each academic day.

Early in the year, the Phonics/Spelling homework assignments are simply tests given by a parent and requiring the parent's signature in the student's notebook. This procedure needs to be established firmly from the beginning. You may wish to explain this procedure during parent-teacher conferences or in a letter sent home to each parent.

In Lesson 67, the structural emphasis is *nouns that form plurals with s* and the vocabulary emphasis is *plants*. After the chart was developed, the students chose words to use in a *paragraph*. The words circled in Figure 2–8 were the words that one student chose to spell. The test was taken on another paper and filed. The homework assignment was to make a *list of any plants in or around the home*, and put the list in *alphabetical order*. One parent's signature is at the bottom of the page.

Throughout each step of the Phonics/Spelling instruction, students are encouraged to think rather than having the teacher identify elements and present them to the students.

THE CYCLES

As shown earlier in this chapter, the vocabulary emphases are grouped into six cycles, each emphasizing different areas of vocabulary development. The cycles have two major purposes:

1. To afford a developmental sequence that introduces new topics as the year proceeds.
2. To provide the opportunity to move from introductory work to more advanced and in-depth work and study within each cycle.

Students progress in spelling ability, knowledge about assorted academic and nonacademic topics, writing, and thinking skills. Although each cycle encompasses different themes and study foci, reviews of items from preceding cycles can be incorporated in any cycle.

Changes in Emphases of Cycles

Notice that the vocabulary, spelling, and structural emphases change with cycle changes as the year progresses. A spelling emphasis is suggested in Cycle 1 (Part 2), Cycle 4, and Cycle 6. The spelling emphasis calls attention to the sequence of certain letters as found in words. Students learn to deal with the specific letter combinations as applied to different words, *not* as a learned specific sound. (Example: end*ing*, *in*struction, l*ine*).

On the other hand, the major emphasis in Cycles 2, 3, and 5 changes from the students' spelling words associated with various letter combinations to students noting the structure of words, such as words containing *prefixes*.

Special attention is given in Cycle 3 to the changes a particular prefix or suffix makes when added to a base or root word. Later in Cycle 5 students apply and relate the knowledge of structural changes as additional prefixes and suffixes are presented with a certain vocabulary focus.

Cycle 1, Parts 1 and 2: Introductory Discussions and Current Events Vocabulary, Lessons 1–60

This first cycle emphasizes discussing and spelling words associated with current events that are

21

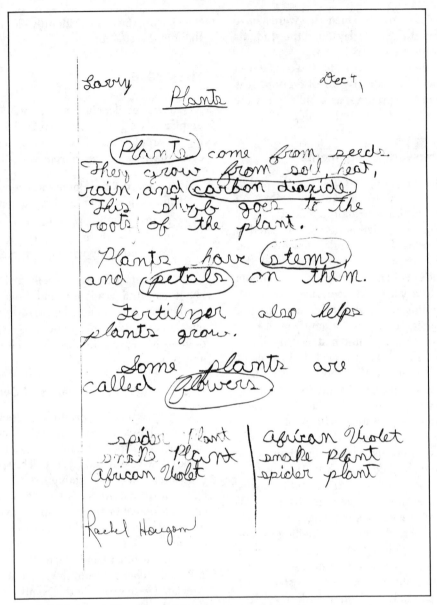

**FIGURE 2–8   Student's Paper Showing In-Class Writing, Words for
Spelling Test, and Parent's Signature**

located in a variety of printed materials, especially newspapers and magazines. This does not mean that topics or words other than those associated with current events will not be volunteered by students during Cycle 1. The emphasis is intended only to give conversational direction and spelling focus for a period of time.

The first ten lessons, of Part 1 of Cycle 1, establish the procedure for the module. These lessons include a vocabulary emphasis as a basis for discussion. They do not contain a spelling emphasis. Beginning with Part 2 of the cycle, in Lesson 11, the students are familiar with the procedure to the extent a spelling emphasis is added.

Figure 2–9 is an example of a class chart developed during Cycle 1. The chart is from Phonics/Spelling Lesson 11, and is included here to illustrate the kinds of words selected by one class during the first cycle. These were words found in *magazines*.

Notice the variation in the difficulty of the words

gr - spelling emphasis — *people*

photograph	great
graduate	agree
geographic	program
autograph	grain
graphite	grandfather
grain	ground
graceful	groovy
grasshopper	gravity
greetings	green
geography	gram
kilogram	gravy

FIGURE 2–9 Phonics/Spelling Class Chart from Lesson 11, Cycle 1

in this chart. Students who can learn words such as *geographic* and *graphite* will have that opportunity. Students who need a more basic spelling vocabulary list will find words such as *grain, ground,* and *great* challenging. All students are focusing on the same letter combination (not sound of letters), in words of their own selection.

Cycle 2: Academic Vocabulary with Structural Emphasis, Lessons 61–90

This cycle affords a change in emphasis to words associated with content area subjects, especially mathematics, social studies, science, etc. For example, on some days within Cycle 2, students volunteer words related to various aspects of mathematics, such as *money, time,* and *geometry,* followed by days when the emphasis is on science-related words, such as *space* and *electricity.*

The basic procedure of students volunteering words containing a specific spelling combination and/ or discussing whether or not these words relate to a topic does not change with any cycle change. This is

one of the parts of the *Success* program that is designed to help students improve their thinking skills.

Each day in Cycle 2 a different structural element, such as a prefix or a suffix is added to the module. As students volunteer the words related to academic vocabulary, you should note with the class any that can be used with the structural element suggested for that module. For example, if the structural element is the suffix *ed,* and a student volunteers the word *date* during a discussion of words associated with the vocabulary emphasis of *time,* note that adding the suffix *ed* changes the spelling and meaning of the word *date.* Write the words both with and without the structural element on the chalkboard and *circle* the structural element.

Example:

Each academic content related word does not have to have the structural element of the module; however, try to write at least one word containing the structural element on the chart each day during Cycle 2.

Figure 2–10 is an example of a class chart developed during Cycle 2. The students used science related materials to locate words they associated with *medicine,* and the structural element was the suffix *ist.* The chart is included to illustrate the kinds of words volunteered in one class on one day during this cycle.

Cycle 3: Linguistic/Structural Emphasis Study, Lessons 91–110

In Cycle 3, the emphasis is on identifying unique kinds of words in the language, such as *synonyms* and *homonyms,* as well as structural aspects of words, such as *prefixes, syllabication,* and *compound words.* In this cycle no specific printed material is suggested for each module because students will need to associate many words with reference to their construction or internal meaning, and it takes too long to locate words with specific elements in a newspaper, for example.

23

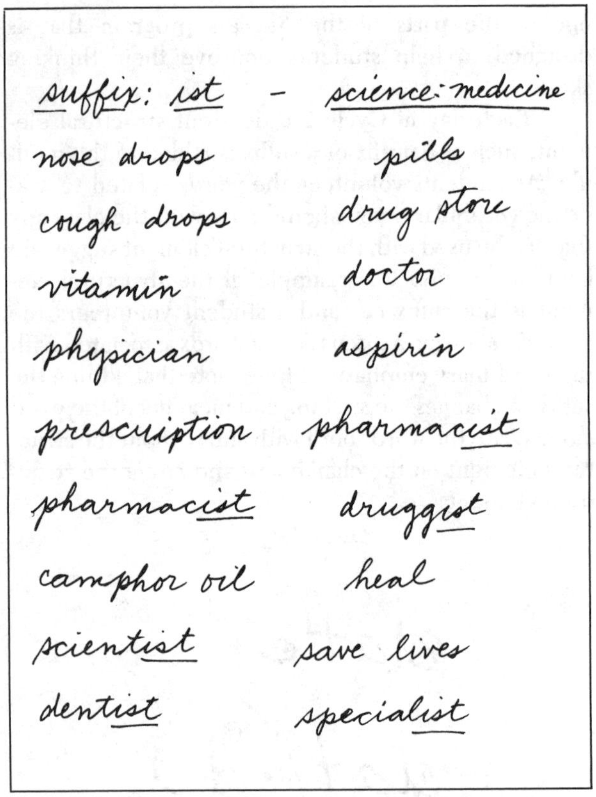

FIGURE 2–10   Phonics/Spelling Class Chart from Lesson 69

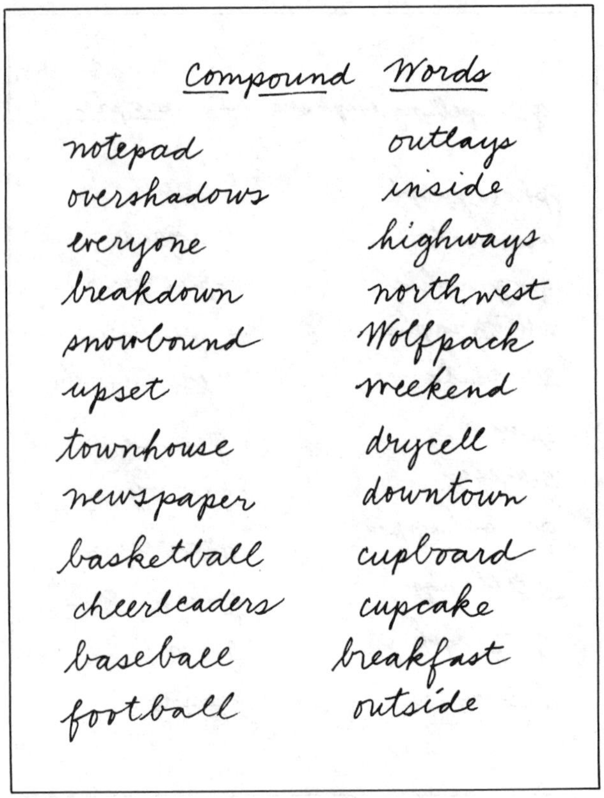

FIGURE 2–11   Phonics/Spelling Class Chart from Lesson 95, Cycle 3

Printed materials may be used for students to locate a word; however, other words of the same type, such as words with the same prefix will need to be volunteered orally by students without having to take time to search for them in books, newspapers, or magazines. There is no vocabulary emphasis in Cycle 3.

Figure 2–11 is an example of a class chart developed during Cycle 3 in Lesson 95, where the word focus was *compound words* with no particular vocabulary emphasis.

Cycle 4: Functional Words with Spelling Emphasis, Lessons 111–125

A theme is suggested for each Phonics/Spelling Module in Cycle 4. Although themes, such as *careers* and *government*, are suggested as discussion guides, there is no suggested kind of printed material for students to use in this cycle as there isn't in Cycle 3. The major emphasis in Cycle 4 is to afford students oppor-

tunities to talk about real-life or functional words they encounter in their lives (*refrigerator, bill*, etc.) and probably will need to know how to spell.

The students should volunteer the words with your assistance. In this cycle, as in all other cycles, you should not prepare a list of words to give to the students for any of the Functional Words Modules in Cycle 4. A spelling emphasis is included in each Cycle 4 Module. Some of these emphases are reviews.

Figure 2–12 is an example of a class chart developed during Cycle 4 in Phonics/Spelling Lesson 124. On this day, students volunteered words they associated with *civil preparedness*. Some of the words contained the spelling emphasis for that module, *em*.

This chart illustrates the tremendous amount of knowledge students have about a given subject. Students are eager to volunteer words and to learn to spell words, when the words are a part of their speaking vocabulary and when the words deal with meaningful subject matter.

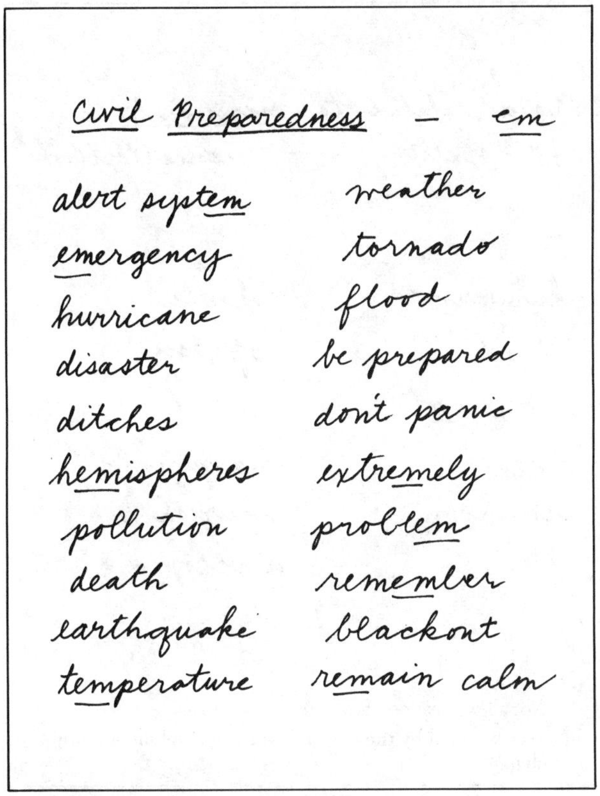

FIGURE 2–12 **Phonics/Spelling Class Chart from Lesson 124, Cycle 4**

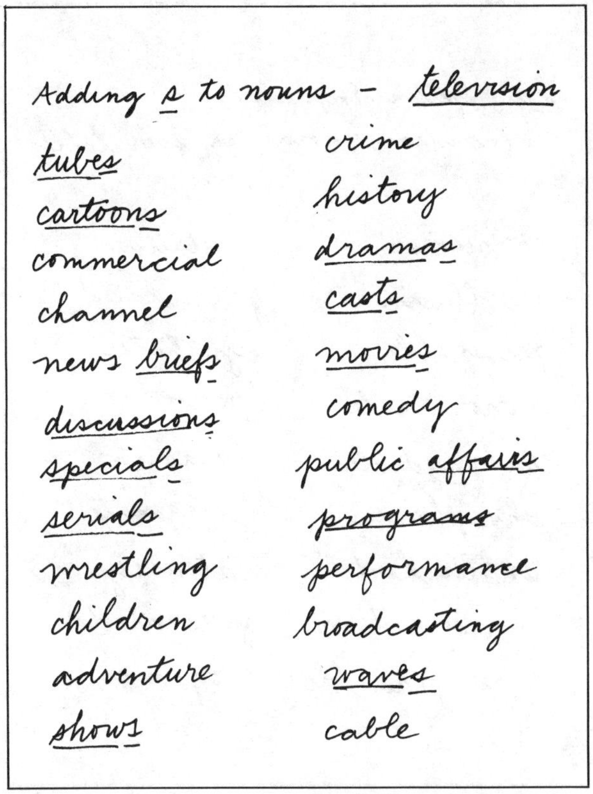

Civil Preparedness — em

alert system	weather
emergency	tornado
hurricane	flood
disaster	be prepared
ditches	don't panic
hemispheres	extremely
pollution	problem
death	remember
earthquake	blackout
temperature	remain calm

FIGURE 2–13 **Phonics/Spelling Class Chart from Lesson 128, Cycle 5**

Adding s to nouns — television

tubes	crime
cartoons	history
commercial	dramas
channel	casts
news briefs	movies
discussions	comedy
specials	public affairs
serials	programs
wrestling	performance
children	broadcasting
adventure	waves
shows	cable

Cycle 5: Recreation Words with Structural Emphasis, Lessons 126–140

Cycle 5 emphasizes words associated with *sports, hobbies, television,* etc. These are words that people use when making their own lists, writing letters to friends, etc., to reveal things they like to do for relaxation or recreation. Again, in Cycle 5, there is no suggested printed material to use as a springboard for locating words, although books, magazines, newspapers, travel folders, or catalogues can be used effectively during Cycle 5. There is a different structural emphasis in each module in Cycle 5. Some of these are reviews.

Figure 2–13 is an example of a class chart developed during Cycle 5 in Phonics/Spelling Lesson 128. On this day, students located words they associated with *television.* The structural emphasis was nouns made plural by adding *s.* Note the variety of words on the chart.

Cycle 6: Expanding Vocabulary with Spelling Emphasis, Lessons 141–180

This cycle emphasizes students volunteering *unfamiliar* words they find in a variety of materials. A different kind of printed material is suggested for each day during this cycle. Essentially, this means students may volunteer words they don't know how to pronounce or define. They may need to spell the words they cannot pronounce as you write them on the chart, and there is a specific spelling emphasis in this cycle. None of these are reviews.

The chart development technique remains the same; however, the discussion of the words located by the students will need to be dealt with in more detail using context clues and dictionaries. The number of words selected by each student will vary from module to module and from cycle to cycle because of the need for time to locate and/or discuss meanings of some words, especially those unfamiliar to the students. The main point is for students to have specific opportuni-

25

hy - Spelling Emphasis
Unfamiliar words on food labels

consumer	nutrition
riboflavin	granulated
perishable	synthetic
mononitrate	pekoe
carbohydrates	thiamin
phosphorus	hydrogenated
unbleached	category
correspondence	federated
biodegradable	organic

FIGURE 2–14 **Phonics/Spelling Class Chart from Lesson 156, Cycle 6**

Words related to *marsupials*
oo - spelling — science textbooks

kangaroo	koala
food	opossum
bandicoot	pouch
moon *	mammal **
raccoon	nourish **
	develop **

*Not all words need to relate to marsupials.
**Words added by the teacher; words not volunteered by students.

FIGURE 2–15 **Phonics/Spelling Class Chart Adapting Lesson 45 to Content Area Instruction**

ties to expand their vocabulary with understanding and improvements in communication skills.

Figure 2–14 is an example of a class chart developed during Phonics/Spelling Lesson 156, Cycle 6. Students found unfamiliar words on *food labels*, and at least one word had the spelling emphasis of *hy*.

By comparing the different charts included in this section of the chapter, it is apparent that there is a tremendous variety of vocabulary development in this part of the Phonics/Spelling Module. There is no controlled vocabulary in the *Success* program; instead, students are encouraged to try to read anything they encounter in print.

CORRELATING CONTENT AREA INSTRUCTION WITH THE PHONICS/SPELLING MODULE

Specific instruction in such areas as mathematics, social studies, science, or health, may take place at other times during the day, or the content area lessons may be taught during the Phonics/Spelling Module. For example, if your class is studying *marsupials* in science, you may use the students' science textbooks and/or other materials containing information on *marsupials* instead of the reference material suggested in that day's Phonics/Spelling Module. The vocabulary emphasis could thus be *marsupials*. Words that you write on the chart paper would be those the students locate in the textbook that they feel are important concerning the topic, have difficulty spelling or pronouncing, or do not know the meanings. You can supplement the list with additional words you want the class to know about the topic. The discussion about marsupials may cease at this time and be continued at a later time designated for science study or may continue during the remainder of the Phonics/Spelling Module.

Figure 2–15 is an example of a class chart resulting from the adaptation of Lesson 45 to coordinate

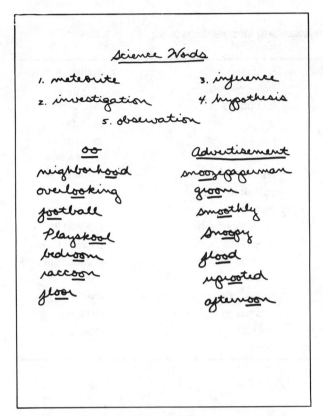

FIGURE 2–16 Phonics/Spelling Class Chart from Lesson 45, Variation 2 of Content Area Chart

with a science lesson on *marsupials*.

A variation of the adaptation by a different teacher is found in Figure 2–16. The spelling emphasis, *oo*, and the vocabulary emphasis, *advertisements*, were not changed. The association of advertising words containing *oo* spelling was made orally as students volunteered some words. The science words were selected by the teacher from a unit being taught during a different part of the day in a science lesson. These science words were written on the chart at the beginning of the Phonics/Spelling Module, and these words were discussed as they were put on the chart. This is another way to correlate language arts and content area lessons.

The Vocabulary/Discussion Emphases

Tables 2–2 and 2–3 list the selected vocabulary emphases or discussion topics for the first and second half of the academic year suggested for inclusion in the Phonics/Spelling Module of the *Success* daily lessons. The lists should be helpful to teachers in planning topics for discussion, reading, writing, and spelling, not only during the *Success* modules, but also during other parts of the school day.

By incorporating a spelling and/or structural emphasis in conjunction with a topic, an additional correlation is found in the Phonics/Spelling Module. Table 2–4 is a partial list of the spelling and structural emphases. The list should be helpful to teachers in planning.

Adaptation of specific topics within the modules does not detract from the base structure of the module. Instead, it brings together different areas of the curriculum and increases the meaning and purpose of the instruction. An additional benefit is that time is saved, and this is very important considering the many topics that need to be covered in the fourth grade curriculum.

USE OF VARIOUS PRINTED MATERIALS

The kinds of printed materials used by the students change in the Phonics/Spelling Modules. For example, the charts from both Phonics/Spelling Modules Lessons 19 and 31 contained words students found in *newspapers*, and Figure 2–17 shows a class chart developed in a fourth grade class during Lesson 52. Students used *magazines* to locate words containing the *er* spelling.

Different printed materials are used in some of the Phonics/Spelling Modules throughout the year to provide a variety of printed materials in addition to the textbooks traditionally found in fourth grade classrooms as a part of the basic curriculum resources. In addition, students learn not only how to locate information, but also that there is science, social studies, mathematics, and other content area information in printed materials other than the traditional content area textbooks.

The dictionary is used extensively in the Phonics/Spelling Module. In fact, most teachers find they, as well as their students, need to consult dictionaries frequently during this module. You are strongly encouraged to look up unfamiliar words while developing the charts to confirm spellings. It is good for students to observe you using a dictionary and could be an opportunity for informal instruction in dictionary skills.

TABLE 2–2 Selected Vocabulary Emphases in the Phonics/Spelling Module, Lessons 1–90, First Half of the Academic Year

school	places	hobbies	editorials
rules	weather	conservation	energy
manners	entertainment	computers	machines
behavior	travel	art	comics
safety	education	nature	accidents
library	medicine	television	government
seasons	people in the news	community affairs	employment
vacations	advertisements	pollution	business
sports	issues	globes	current events
transportation	national events	important events	colonial life
vocations	food	musicians	popular music
health	positive topics	musical instruments	parts of the body
world affairs	money	nutrition	personal hygiene
public announcements	measurement	body systems	time
recreation	plants	geometry	numbers
economics	space	animals	land types
maps	bodies of water	cities	

TABLE 2–3 Selected Vocabulary Emphases in the Phonics/Spelling Module, Lessons 91–180, Second Half of the Academic Year

synonyms	journals	transportation-related words
homonyms	recreation-related words	seasonal-related words
compound words	bicycles	citizenship
multiple meanings	clubs/organization	shopping-related words
suffixes	vacations	sports-related words
safety-related words	sports	fiction
home-related words	antonyms	water-related words
health care	contractions	camping-related words
communication-related words	syllabication	games
civil preparedness	prefixes	seasonal games
disasters	careers	hobbies
television-related words	government-related words	

(In Cycle 6, expanding vocabulary with a spelling emphasis, students locate unfamiliar words in the following materials, instead of words that refer to a vocabulary/discussion topic.)

newspapers	dictionaries	science textbooks
magazines	spelling textbooks	mathematics textbooks
telephone books	music textbooks	health textbooks
labels	social studies textbooks	
encyclopedias	language textbooks	

TABLE 2–4   Selected List of Spelling and Structural Emphases in the Phonics/Spelling Module

(NOTE: The Following are Considered Minimum. You May Wish to Add Additional Items.)

gr	cl	y	in	re	tr	ve	cy
pr	tr	ai	tion	sub	nt	ry	ap
gl	wh	aw	ness	ex	spl	rt	tw
fl	ch	qu	inter	ment	spr	ff	rl
sm	th	er	ly	ing	nk	iz	sis
sc	sh	in	ing	ful	em	wn	sne
fr	br	ur	pre	sion	nd	rc	url
sk	pl	ir	un	tion	ses	rk	flo
sp	al	an	dis	ly	er	po	opt
st	ck	l	ful	less	s	dy	eg
dr	ee	es	ian	al	ed	gth	cyc
sw	ea	ss	ed	ng	able	mb	exp
ance	i	ment	ous	thr	be	syn	ght
bl	e	milli	un	or	de	hy	spa
fr	a	ty	in	sn	er	iv	zu
str	o	un	im	sl	est	mp	bom
dw	oo	ish	dis	gh	ure	nt	hyp
tw	oa		pre		ph	eye	nst
st	u						ric

Learning to effectively read, write, and spell words from many kinds of printed resources is a built-in feature of the *Success* program. In the Phonics/Spelling Module, encyclopedias, labels, etc., are valuable resources; however, this does not minimize the importance of textbooks and reference materials in the module.

SUMMARY OF PHONICS/SPELLING MODULES STRUCTURE

For approximately 30–40 minutes each day, time should be allocated for:

1. Discussion of a particular topic and spelling emphasis or structural emphasis and students to locate in newspapers, magazines, textbooks, etc., words related to the discussion.

2. Teachers to write on chart paper words associated with the theme(s) discussed and underline the spelling or structural emphasis indicated for the module.

3. Students to write information concerning the theme(s) and select words to study for the spelling test.

4. Teachers to move around the classroom during the writing and spelling study time and help individual students at their desks.

5. A spelling test by each pair of students given orally or written and checked by the student's partner.

6. The paper to be dated and filed either in the student's folder or in a spiral-bound notebook. The folder or notebook, when filled, is kept in a box labeled *Phonics/Spelling Papers* until the end of the academic year. At the end of the year the notebooks or folders are sent home.

u

every	Carter
November	southern
laser	personal
operation	everywhere
Denver	kernel
superintendent	government
Speigner	northern
manager	barbershop

FIGURE 2–17 **Phonics/Spelling Class Chart from Lesson 52**

vocabulary chart.

Do not omit the Phonics/Spelling Module. It is important for students to have opportunities to use their vocabulary in conjunction with content area topics as well as to learn specialized terminology and concepts as they study spelling and writing. In addition, they need opportunities such as those provided in this module to associate a variety of topics with printed information in a variety of materials. During this module, students are encouraged to think through and to apply information, rather than being spoon-fed. Improved thinking skills are an especially exciting by-product of this module.

7. The chart produced during the module to be displayed in the classroom for at least two weeks. After two weeks, approximately ten charts are displayed in the classroom. The oldest charts are removed as new charts are developed for display and for use as resource materials for the students. Charts may be displayed by months and kept up in the classroom for the entire year.

8. A homework assignment made by the teacher, to be completed in the student's spiral notebook and signed by a parent.

Figure 2–18 is an example taken from the Phonics/Spelling Module, Cycle 5, Lesson 138 (vocabulary emphasis, *vacations*; structural emphasis, *ing* form of verbs). It illustrates the development of the class

ing - verbs - vacation word

playing	being lazy
camping	diving
having fun	hiking
visiting	backpacking
swimming	mountains
sleeping bag	climbing
cookouts	running
staking	hitting balls
catching fish	wading
cottage	collecting
beach	people
sunshine	making friend
sleeping late	fishing

FIGURE 2–18 **Phonics/Spelling Class Chart from Lesson 138, Cycle 5**

References

Anderson, Paul S., and Diane Lapp. *Language Skills in Elementary Education.* New York: Macmillan, 1979.

Burns, Paul C., and Betty L. Broman. *The Language Arts in Childhood Education.* Chicago: Rand McNally, 1979.

Dale, Edgar, and Joseph O'Rourke. *Techniques of Teaching Vocabulary.* Palo Alto: Field Education Publications, 1971.

Deighton, Lee C. *Vocabulary Development in the Classroom.* New York: Teachers College Press, Columbia University, 1959.

Holmes, Stewart W. *Meaning in Language.* New York: Harcourt Brace Jovanovich, 1972.

Smith, Frank. *Understanding Reading.* New York: Holt, Rinehart and Winston, 1978.

Spache, George D., and Evelyn B. Spache. *Reading in the Elementary School,* 3rd ed. Boston: Allyn and Bacon, 1973.

chapter three
How to Teach the Composition Module

The second 30 minutes of each lesson are devoted to the correlation of reading, writing, spelling, listening, and thinking, with an emphasis on students writing about topics familiar to them. The Composition Modules are found in the second column in Appendix One. Although the time suggested is an approximation, the students should receive a *minimum* of 30 minutes of writing instruction each day.

RATIONALE

This module affords you opportunities to *respond* to the students' written language and thought processes, rather than merely checking for errors in writing. For example, instead of being concerned that a student cannot define an *adverbial phrase*, see if the student can use an adverbial phrase in his or her own writing.

Learning the process of written expression receives priority over details of grammar and style. Many students have "turned-off" to writing extensively because they were asked to concentrate on minute mistakes before they were able to express their thoughts. In the Composition Modules, each student should be treated as an individual, with your comments being directed toward *what that student has written or plans to write* in an immediate situation. The objective is to help students improve their written expression while learning writing skills. Students need to grasp not just what an adjective is, but the concept that there are words that can be used to clarify other words. Refining student writing should not be given priority over learning to write. Many students can write excellent short stories before they learn technical grammatical terminology.

Unfortunately, in the past, some classes have offered a hodgepodge of composition-related activities that often were frustrating to both teacher and students. The spelling words for the Friday spelling test, for example, usually were unrelated to other language arts lessons, and some words may not even have been in the students' working vocabulary. The stories selected for reading lessons frequently had little to do with writing assignments. Students moved from assignment to assignment and the label "busy work" came into being as a part of the school day. This approach is neither realistic nor is it educationally sound. Sadly, in some instances, students spent so much time completing activities related to a single specific skill that they had little time to read or write on their own.

The *Success* program provides both structure and flexibility for combining mechanics and content. In this module, for example, the teacher may comment to one student about a word that needs to be spelled correctly and a sentence that might be improved by adding a comma series. When the teacher works with another student during the same

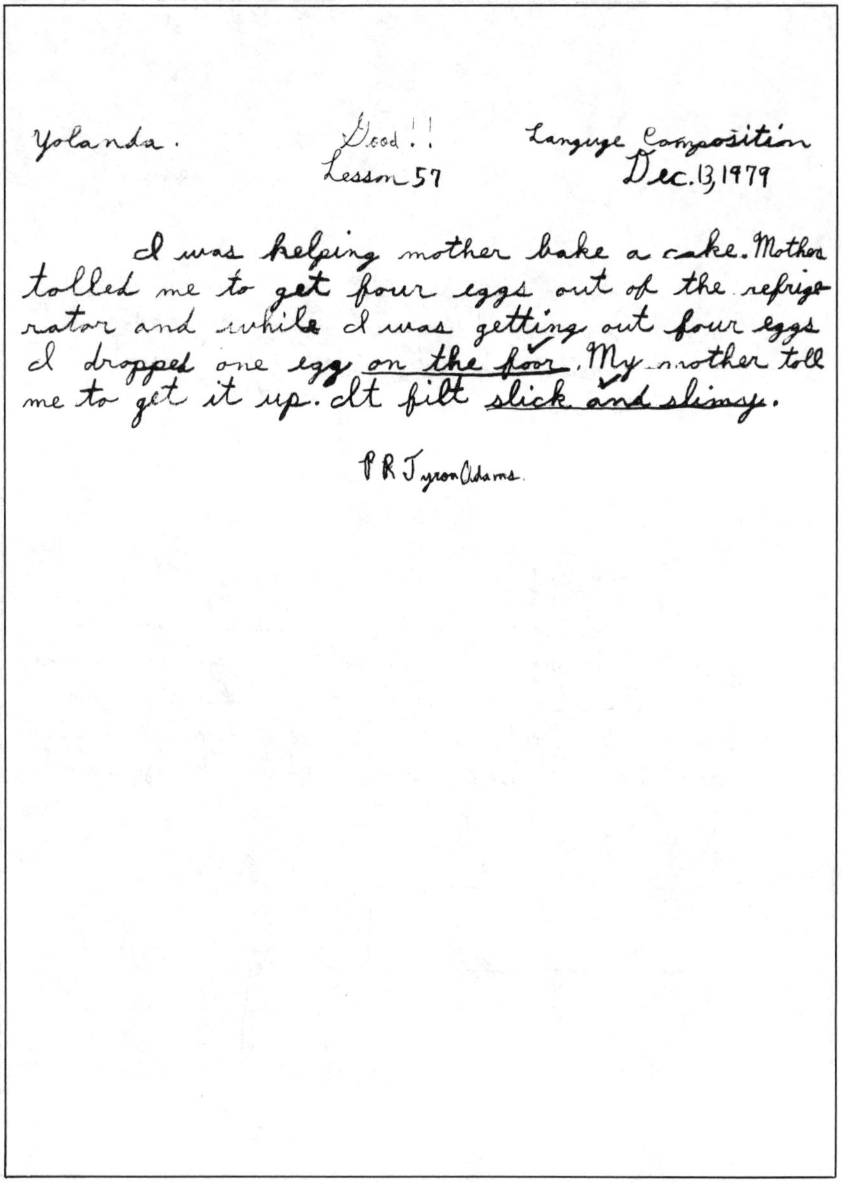

> Yolanda.   Good!!   Langusge Composition
>   Lesson 57   Dec. 13, 1979
>
>   I was helping mother bake a cake. Mother
> tolled me to get four eggs out of the refrige-
> rator and while I was getting out four eggs
> I dropped one egg on the floor. My mother toll
> me to get it up. It filt slick and slimey.
>
>   P R Tyron Adams.

FIGURE 3–1   Student's Writing During Lesson 57—Including Prepositional Phrases in an Assigned Topic

module, the comments might be about improving the clarity of a cause and effect situation and inserting a comma. *The focus depends on what the student has written or plans to write*, rather than on predetermined items that may not be useful to the student at all.

There is a delicate balance between helping students improve *mechanics* without stifling the creativity of their written expression. Rather than a haphazard approach, each day has one definite *proofreading*

thrust for the student to concentrate on for improving his or her writing skills. The proofreading thrusts call attention to mechanics, such as punctuation, or to content, such as inclusion of adjectives. The object of each module, however, is not to overemphasize a proofreading thrust, but to give directional emphasis to encourage the student in clarity and correctness of written self-expression.

Figure 3–1 illustrates the concept discussed in the above paragraph. The student's assignment in Les-

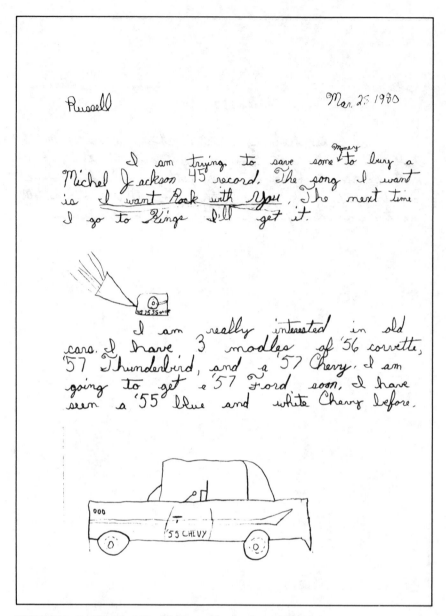

Russell   Mar. 25 1980

I am trying to save some money to buy a Michel Jackson 45 record. The song I want is *I want Rock with You*. The next time I go to Kings I'll get it.

I am really interested in old cars. I have 3 modles of '56 corvette, '57 Thunderbird, and a '57 Chevy. I am going to get a '57 Ford soon. I have seen a '55 blue and white Chevy before.

'55 CHEVY

FIGURE 3–2 Student A's Writing—No Assigned Theme

son 57 was to write about the topic "slick and slimy" and to include in the writing at least one prepositional phrase denoting position. There is a definite sense of the "slick and slimy" concept in the paper and the student was able to include the prepositional phrase. There are, however, errors in the paper such as the misspelled words *felt* and *told*. If the teacher goes overboard in trying to extract a "perfect" paper from this fourth grader at this particular time during the day, some of the concept development may be lost.

This, as well as other compositions written by students during this module, will be filed and students will have access to them. Perhaps later during the year they may spot some errors made in earlier papers and correct them. If not, they have many years of education ahead of them. At least, at this point they are writing and are not afraid to try to write.

Most modules afford guidance for students in

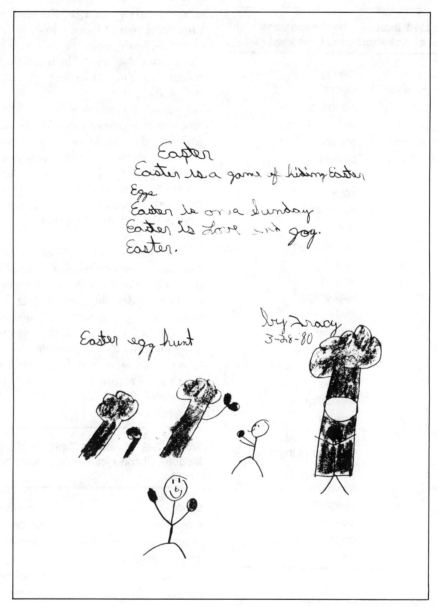

FIGURE 3–3   Student B's Writing—No Assigned Theme

developing thematic content; however, some modules have no themes and students may write about any topic of interest to them. In either instance, the vocabulary comes from the students, not a predetermined word listing or a "handwriting" book where the students copy model words and paragraphs.

Figures 3–2, 3–3, and 3–4 are student compositions showing examples of the variety of writing that students produce on a "free writing" day when no

theme is suggested by the teacher. The students wrote about any topic of interest to them. The teacher and students decided there would be no particular proofreading thrust for the writings on this day.

Daily writing (a minimum of 30 minutes), a variety of academic and nonacademic themes as well as no thematic assignments, insertion of a specific proofreading thrust in almost every Composition Module, and a variety of writing assignments work

TABLE 3–1 Selected Topics in the Composition Module, First Half of Academic Year, Lessons 1–90

description of people	reality
daily and weekly schedules	humor
food	elephants
school subjects	fright
objectives in the classroom	snakes
motorcycles	planets
bicycles	occupations
pumpkins	colors
animals	desks and chairs
telephone	underwater
leaves	time changes
sun and moon	nature
frustration	actions
characters	family trips
football season	birds
kites	inventions
dinosaurs	slimy things
self	prehistoric times
dreams	turkeys
sports	friendship
hobbies	movies
favoritism	pets
frogs	seasons of the year
invitation to a party	cafeteria
letters to the editor	concerns
race cars	spaghetti
clowns	country life
sharks	snow
	gifts

together to help each student improve his or her writing ability in both content and mechanics. The following procedure is extremely important in predicting success in writing across the curriculum during an academic year.

CONTENT OF WRITING EMPHASIS

In the Composition Module, each student writes an original item daily—story, sentence, poem, memo—using words of his or her own selection. Students do not copy information, although they might use some of the words written on the chalkboard during the prewriting part of this module.

There are major or umbrella *themes* identified throughout the year, which are open-ended so each student can think of writing content that is related to the theme.

Some themes have suggested subthemes. These give some degree of focus for discussion and writing with reference to the umbrella theme.

The writing topics in the lessons change daily to afford a variety of suggestions; however, you may decide to continue the same topic for more than one day. A third possibility is to substitute the suggested writing theme with a topic emphasized during another part of the day.

The student example which follows (Figure 3–5) illustrates how one teacher modified a lesson so that the students could write about a recent field trip. The teacher decided the proofreading thrust would be to include a *proper noun* in the composition.

The Composition Module alone in the *Success* program contains a large variety of suggested writing themes. These range from traditional themes for fourth graders (*prehistoric times*) to uncommon topics (*desks and chairs*). Table 3–1 lists selected themes or

TABLE 3–2 Selected Topics in the Composition Module, Second Half of Academic Year, Lessons 91–180

space	mysteries
emotions	fantasy
music	scientific information
advertisements	journals
deserts	autobiography
apples	summer
characters	books
teachers	ships
zoo	happy events
animals	tall tales
fables	lyrics
drama	opinions
fame	future
metamorphosis	letters
automobiles	paper plates
formulas	water
	wild horses

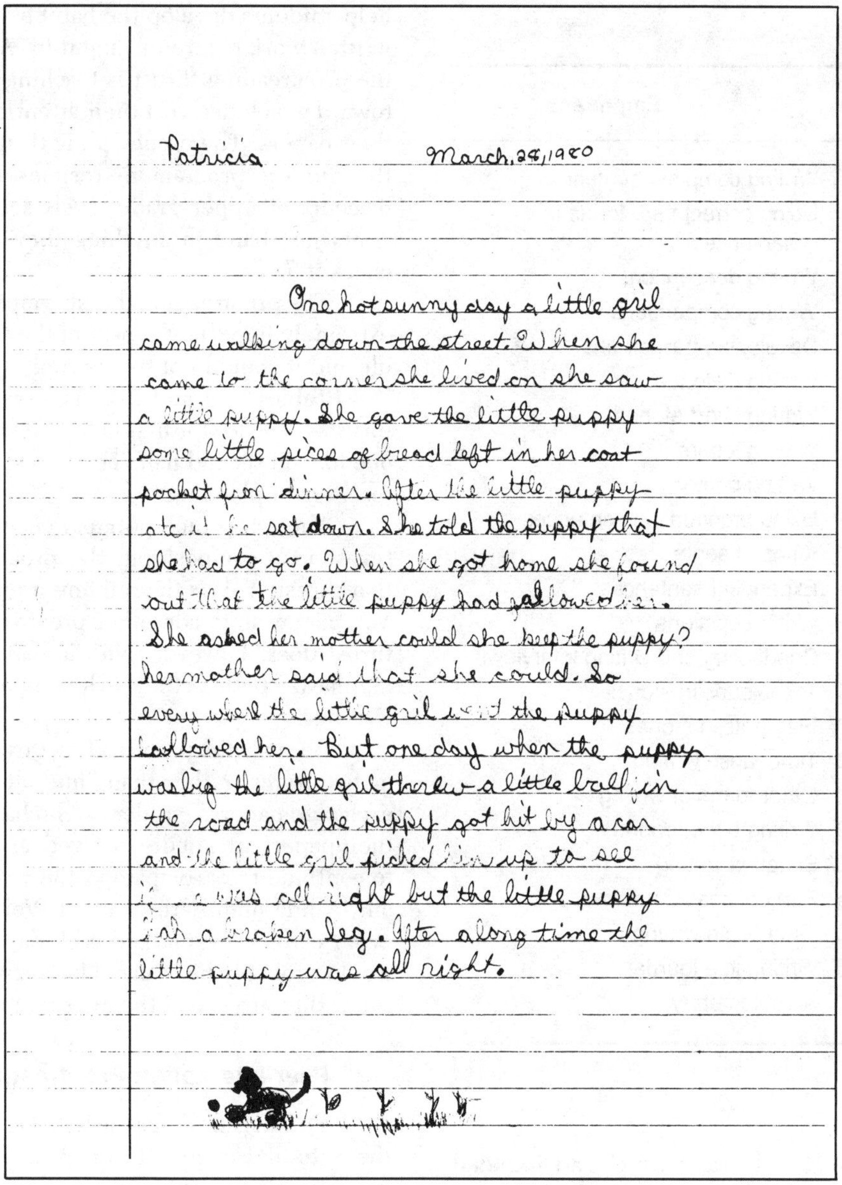

Patricia   March 24, 1980

One hot sunny day a little girl
came walking down the street. When she
came to the corner she lived on she saw
a little puppy. She gave the little puppy
some little pices of bread left in her coat
pocket from dinner. After the little puppy
ate it he sat down. She told the puppy that
she had to go. When she got home she found
out that the little puppy had followed her.
She asked her mother could she keep the puppy?
her mother said that she could. So
every where the little girl went the puppy
followed her. But one day when the puppy
was big the little girl threw a little ball in
the road and the puppy got hit by a car
and the little girl picked him up to see
if he was all right but the little puppy
had a broken leg. After a long time the
little puppy was all right.

FIGURE 3–4   Student C's Writing—No Assigned Theme

knowledge area topics suggested for discussion prior to student writing in the Composition Module. These should be helpful in planning for the entire academic year. You may wish to vary the topics and/or add others. Additional knowledge area topics are found in the Phonics/Spelling and Study Skills Modules.

There are writing topics that are suited for completely imaginary kinds of writing. Figure 3–6, a paper written during Lesson 6, illustrates imaginary focus rather than academic or factual. In Lesson 6, each student develops sentences and/or a paragraph about a pet dinosaur as an imaginary character. The students checked closely for all sentences to begin with a *capital letter* and end with *proper punctuation*, which was the proofreading thrust for this particular day.

TABLE 3–3

Cycle	Lesson	Emphases
1	1–10	Writing complete sentences
2	11–20	Using correct verb forms in sentences
3	21–25	Writing descriptions
4	26–30	Writing comparisons
5	31–40	Developing paragraphs
6	41–50	Writing dialogue
7	51–60	Writing short stories
8	61–70	Writing letters
9	71–80	Writing poetry
10	81–90	Using pronouns in sentences
11	91–95	Kinds of sentences
12	96–100	Expanding sentences
13	101–105	Writing opinions
14	106–110	Conducting and writing interviews
15	111–124	Techniques in stories
16	125–130	Elements in stories
17	131–135	Time-lapse writing
18	136–144	Other forms of writing
19	145–149	Writing book reports
20	150–160	Situation writing
21	161–165	Parts of speech review
22	166–170	Time-lapse writing
23	171–175	Writing in a journal
24	176–180	Autobiography

THE CYCLES

In the Composition Module, various cycles are included to provide students with opportunities to emphasize different kinds of writing, such as dialogues comparisons, and reports. Table 3–3 is a list of the Composition cycles and the lessons in which each cycle is emphasized.

MECHANICS OF WRITING EMPHASES

The Proofreading Thrusts

Most Composition Modules contain a suggested proofreading thrust, the major purpose of which is to help students develop the habit of self-checking their written work before turning it in. Another purpose of the proofreading thrust is teaching students specifics toward which to direct their attention while rereading their papers. The proofreading thrusts were built into the *Success* program in response to comments by teachers at upper grade levels such as, "Many students just hand in anything they write. They don't check it."

The proofreading thrust, emphasized daily, is an extremely important aspect of the Composition Module and it should not be omitted.

Tables 3–4 and 3–5 list selected proofreading thrusts—one for the first half of the academic year and one for the second half. The lists should be helpful to teachers in planning.

The writer incorporates *at least one* proofreading thrust in a composition; the proofreader checks for that thrust. This is the minimum proofreading thrust. You may wish to add other proofreading thrusts. The thrust does, however, offer a lead-in for students to emphasize both as they write and as they check their writings.

Because the proofreading thrust is limited to one or two items, rather than "find all errors before you exchange papers," students who have many errors on their papers are not discouraged, and do have a chance to continue to participate in the writing lessons without feeling unduly threatened. For some students, if every error were marked each day, a sense of defeat would probably be realized by many students. Defeat is not the purpose of the *Success* program.

Peer-Interaction Proofreading

For decades, teachers have collected some of their student papers, taken them home, spent hours reading and marking them, and returned the papers. Some students glanced at the marks, and that was about it. The teacher did the proofreading, and few students benefited because they did not go through the process. The practice of teachers taking sets of papers home to grade should not be discontinued entirely; however, there is a need for a method that gives students *daily and immediate feedback* concerning their writing, with the students going through the process. This is one of the purposes of peer-interaction proofreading.

During the proofreading process, each student

has a partner and there must be opportunity for them to talk about their papers. Following is the procedure for peer-interaction proofreading. Steps 1–4, 7, and 8 should be implemented the first day of school. When students understand this technique, add Steps 5 and 6. It will take time for all students to remember and use all of the parts. You may wish to put the following eight steps on a chart until students become accustomed to the proofreading symbols and procedure.

1. The writer makes a check (√) *above at least one example of correct use* of the proofreading thrust. (Every capitalized letter does not need to be checked.)

EXAMPLE: Proofreading thrust—*capitalization*
       √   √
       I live in New york.

2. Students exchange papers for the peer-interaction proofreading session.

TABLE 3–4   Selected Proofreading Thrusts from Lessons 1–90

adjective	interrogative sentences
capitalization	question mark
proper nouns	quotation marks
period	time words
detail	dialogue paragraph change
verb	size words
common nouns	descriptive sentence
subject	exclamatory sentence
predicate	subject/verb agreement
simple subject	verb tenses
pronoun	possessive
punctuation	prepositional phrase
letter formation	adverb
paragraph indention	pronoun/verb agreement
topic sentence	plural subject
comma	singular subject
abbreviation	rhyming words
contraction	job-related words
sentence beginning	poetry forms
simile	

TABLE 3–5   Selected Proofreading Thrusts from Lessons 91–180

plural forms	titles
time words	author's name
use of *a, an, the*	use of *their, there*
comma series	capital *I*
adverbs	simile
adjectives	exclamation mark
capitalization	cause and effect in plot
words denoting persuasion	sentence beginning
description of setting	contraction
sequence	affixes
words denoting fantasy	commas in letters
character description	proper/common nouns
mood words	verb tenses
prefixes	suffixes
run-on sentences	pronouns
prepositional phrases	subject-verb agreement
compound sentences	spelling
possessives	punctuation
character introduction	dialogue
dates	emotion words
cities	states
letter form	imperative sentence with understood *you* as subject
punctuation for dialogue	comparisons
unusual adjectives	relative pronouns—*who, that, which*
notation of sources (page numbers)	superlatives
hyperbole (gross exaggeration)	articles
paragraph organization	sentence fragments
figurative language, metaphors	words to excite reader's curiosity
opinion words	predicate adjectives (after *become, is,* etc.)
"place" words	description of conflict and its resolution
comparison and contrast (parallel structure)	
paragraph indenting	
demostrative (*this, that, these, those*)	

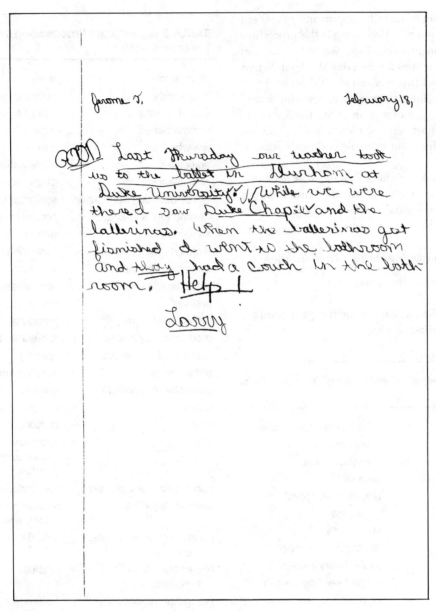

FIGURE 3–5 Modification of a Writing Topic

3. The proofreader makes a check (√) *above each indication of correct use* of the thrust.

EXAMPLE: If the proofreading thrust is capitalization, the proofreader makes a check above each capital letter.

    √√   √√
I live in New york.

4. If found, the proofreader makes an (X) above *at least one proofreading error*.

EXAMPLE: √√   √√ X
I live in New york.

The above illustrates the attention on writing mechanics in the Composition Module. You may wish to add other proofreading thrusts; however, there should be at least one per module.

Attention to *content* during the proofreading part of the module should be developed as follows:

5. The proofreader finds *at least one good writing segment* in the paper and writes GOOD in the left margin on or near the line where it appears. This is a subjective opinion—it can be a word, phrase, sentence, or entire paragraph. The proof-

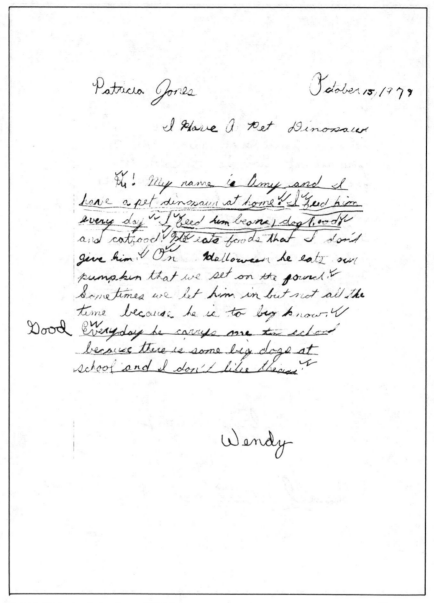

FIGURE 3–6 Imaginary Writing

reader underlines the part considered good.

6. The proofreader writes "HELP" in the left margin beside at least one writing segment that could be improved and underlines twice that word, phrase, or whatever could be improved. There may be other parts to improve; however, the idea is to focus on success through at least one improvement each day.

7. The proofreader writes his or her name at the bottom of the page and returns the paper to the writer for improvements.

8. The writer files the paper on the segment writing days and after more than one day of the time-lapse writing. The writer gives the paper to the teacher on the first day of the time-lapse writing.

Figure 3–7 is a student's paper written in the Composition Module during Lesson 31. The writer wrote a paragraph about a time when she was angry. The proofreader checked for the proofreading thrust (verbs which add *ed* to form the past tense). He also noted that "sadisfide" was misspelled and needed "help." Some changes were made on the paper after

41

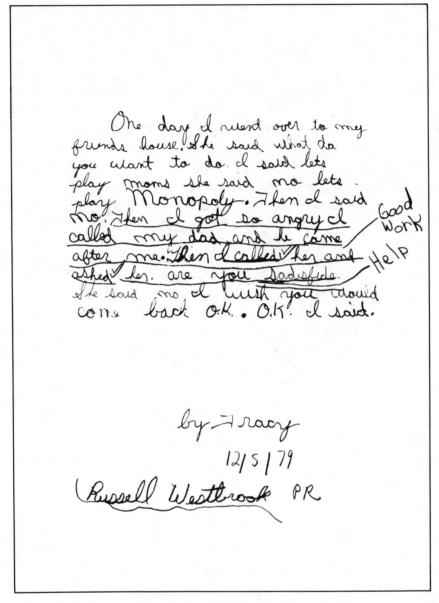

FIGURE 3–7 Proofreading Marks on Writing from Lesson 31

the proofreader and the writer discussed what had been written. Discussion between writer and proofreader clarifies why the proofreader selects certain items to mark and not others.

A variation of the proofreading technique is to have the writer underline or circle the proofreading thrust instead of checking it. The proofreader checks the proofreading thrust. Figure 3–8 is a student composition from Lesson 113 illustrating this technique. The writer circled and labeled a *simile* used in his description of a picture which was on display. The

proofreader checked ($\sqrt{}$) the simile agreeing that it was correct. The proofreading thrust was to use a simile or metaphor or both in the writing. Not only did the writer and proofreader understand similes, but they knew the difference between a simile and a metaphor.

Obviously, other items pertaining to content and/or mechanics will be discussed during the peer-interaction proofreading part of each day's module. Unless absolutely necessary, you should leave defense of writing, incorporation of corrections and changes, etc., to the student writer and proofreader. There is

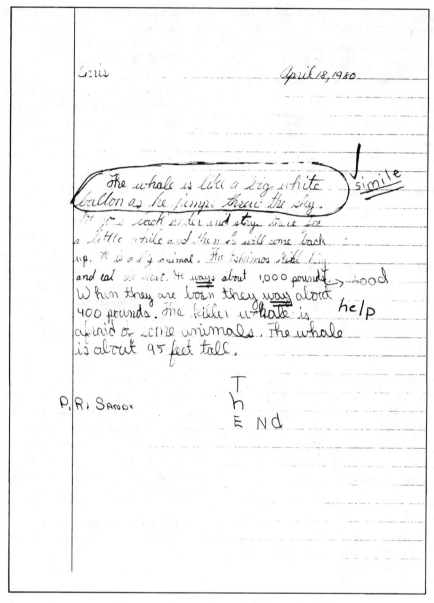

FIGURE 3–8   Proofreading Marks on Writing from Lesson 113

no reason for you to feel that you must read and mark each student's paper each day. Teacher input should be primarily oral with reference to an item just written by the student. The object is to provide time during the academic year for students to grow toward independent writing and proofreading.

Summary of Proofreading Plan

1. Name of proofreader written at top or bottom of page.

2. √ above at least one correct use of the proofreading thrust or underlines an example of the proofreading thrust.

3. X above each error of proofreading thrust.

4. "GOOD" in left or right margin near evidence of a good writing segment.

5. Underline once the writing segment in the that has been judged good.

6. "HELP" written in left or right margin near evidence of poor writing or error in mechanics.

43

7. <u>Underline twice</u> the writing segment in the paper that needs improvement.

8. Student returns paper to the writer who should improve the X areas and the HELP sections before dating and filing the paper in the Composition box.

All Composition Module writings should be filed. Students may find and correct errors in April on papers they wrote in February. The paper does not need to be completely correct before filing; however, if possible the paper should have been improved in some way by the student before filing.

COMPOSITION MODULE TEACHING SEQUENCE

There are six major instructional parts in each Composition Module. When you begin teaching the *Success* program, follow these steps carefully.

1. Have a prewriting discussion with students about the theme of the module. Write the proofreading theme on the board.

2. Note on the chalkboard key words, phrases, or sentences suggested by students during the prewriting discussion. Write on the chalkboard *during* the discussion and not afterwards.

3. Have students write according to your instructions, while you move around the classroom helping individuals at their desks.

4. Have each student proofread another student's paper focusing on the proofreading thrust noted in each lesson of this module.

5. Have each student read his or her paper, or parts of the paper to another student.

6. Have each student date the paper and file it in his or her manila folder in a box labeled *Composition*. The papers do not go home until the end of the year. This is another of the longitudinal records of student progress included in the *Success* program.

Following is a suggested sequence for teaching each of the above six parts of the Composition Module, using the theme *people do different things* and the proofreading thrust of *locating subject and predicate in a sentence*.

First Ten Minutes

1. Write the theme *people do different things* on the chalkboard and write a sentence about that theme. Underline the *subject and predicate* in the sentence and comment briefly on each.

2. Students volunteer additional sentences orally that are associated with the theme of people doing different things. Write each sentence or word cluster on the chalkboard before other words are volunteered. If two or more students write sentences on other parts of the chalkboard while you are writing sentences, more sentences can be written during this part of the module. In each instance, mark the *subject and predicate* on the chalkboard *before* the next sentence is written. All sentences written on the chalkboard should come from students and be associated with the theme.

Write the proofreading thrust suggested for the module in a box on the chalkboard and give one or two examples of the thrust. Do not hold all students back for a lengthy description of the thrust. Additional explanations can be made to individuals who may be having trouble grasping the concept at their desks. Reviews and reinforcements can be made on other days.

Next Fifteen Minutes

3. Students write their name at the top of a sheet of paper, and for approximately ten minutes they write sentences associated with the theme. You should walk around the classroom, stopping to help individual students at their desks and making comments about their writing. You should always begin with a positive comment and then add something that can be improved. As parts of their writing, students can use items written on the chalkboard during the prewriting part of this module and additional ideas related to the theme.

4. On his or her paper, the student puts a check (√) *above* the item on the paper that was requested for the proofreading thrust. In this

example, the check would be placed above *at least one subject and predicate*.

Last Five Minutes

5. Students exchange papers and each student writes his or her name at the *bottom* of a partner's paper, and the initials *PR* after the name to signify he or she is the proofreader.

6. The proofreader puts the second check (√√) beside the writer's check if the writing is correct. If an error is made or the check does not indicate the proofreading thrust, the proofreader places an (X) beside the writer's check. Students should consult dictionaries and other reference materials when questions arise, before asking the teacher.

7. The proofreader locates one part of the paper (choice of a word or phrase, formation of a letter, etc.) and *underlines it once* to indicate an example of good writing and writes GOOD in the left margin near the word, phrase, letter, etc. This can relate to content or mechanics.

8. The proofreader locates one part of the paper (an additional word would clarify meaning, poorly formed letter, absence of capital letter where needed, etc.) and *underlines it twice* to indicate an example of writing that could be improved. The proofreader writes HELP in the left margin near whatever can be improved.

9. The proofreader returns the paper to the writer, and if time allows, the writer should read some or all of the paper to another student.

10. The paper is dated and filed in a box labeled *Composition* and is not sent home until the end of the year.

Occasionally, a homework assignment is suggested in this module. Locate at least one page in a language textbook where there are activities concerning the proofreading thrust (*subject/predicate* in this case) and assign page(s) as homework to reinforces the classwork.

Figure 3–9 is a student paper showing clearly all steps involved in the development of this lesson except words written on the chalkboard during the introductory discussion, and the filing of the paper at the end of the module.

THE FIRST THREE WEEKS OF INSTRUCTION

The Writings

Do not expect "perfect" writing at the beginning of the school year, and do not ask students to copy papers over before filing them in the Composition box. Although there may be many errors on a student's paper, your guideline is to (1) find something in the student's work to compliment him or her about, and (2) follow immediately by pointing to *one* instance of a misspelled word, incorrect grammar, poor letter formation, or need for additional information. Move to another student, repeating the procedure. It is best if the comments refer to a specific item on the student's paper rather than to a series of items. It is better if the student understands exactly how to correct one specific item on his or her paper, than to be confused by having to correct several items. Each day of the academic year will provide opportunities for your additional comments. The comments, however, should be in response to a specific writing sample. Each day, also, will provide opportunities for the students to improve their writing ability.

The Proofreading Thrusts

The entire proofreading plan described in this chapter should not be introduced at one time. *Introduce only one item* of the plan and don't introduce the next part until the students feel comfortable with, and understand, the proofreading techniques already introduced. Once all items or parts of the plan have been introduced, students should be able to complete the proofreading with you saying only the words "Proofreading time." It is suggested that you write the specific proofreading thrust for that day on the chalkboard prior to the beginning of the Composition Module.

TYPES OF WRITING EMPHASES

The two major types of writing emphasized are short-term (segment) and long-term (time-lapse). The first represents on-the-spot writing with little opportunity for revision, and the second represents writing situation where there is time for additions and other revisions.

Segment Writing Modules

The short-term or segment writings are expected to be completed by the end of the 30 minutes. Most of the writing assignments in the Composition Module are segment writings. Although the mode (story, poem, letter) may vary, they are designed to be completed in one day. The manner in which students complete the segment is left to your expertise, depending on your knowledge of individuals in the class. For example, you may assign some students to write *paragraph* segments, while less capable students write *phrases*. This is another aspect of the built-in individualized instruction of the *Success* program.

One purpose of the segment writing is to teach students that some writing situations mandate closure at a specific time. The writing paper filed by the student at the end of the 30 minutes represents his or her complete segment, with no more time to add or revise words. A practical example of this type of writing is when one must write and mail a letter by a time deadline. The procedure is described in the preceding section, "Composition Teaching Sequence."

Figure 3–10 is an example of segment writing. It was written during a 30-minute lesson, proofread, and filed. Lesson 156 has as a proofreading thrust using *if* or *when* to begin a sentence.

Time-Lapse Writing Modules

Sections of the Composition Module are scheduled for time-lapse writing, and represent an important concept. Not all writing is completed at one sitting; therefore, students should develop the habit of adding to their written work on a different day. On one day, the student begins a composition related to a theme. On the following academic day, the student adds to the composition, and if appropriate, revises it. In addition, with at least one night between the writings on the same theme, students begin to think of other items to add to their writing and have an in-school opportunity to expand their initial writing.

The following procedure is suggested for use in teaching the time-lapse writing modules:

1. Either use the theme indicated in the Composition Module for that day, or substitute a topic that can be extended for at least two days.
2. Write the title of the theme and the proofreading thrust on the chalkboard and discuss the topic for approximately five minutes.

3. Write on the chalkboard some of the words, phrases, or sentences related to the topic and *volunteered by the students*. In most instances, students volunteer a variety of words they associate with the topic. If the student can justify a relationship between words volunteered and the topic, accept the student's thinking, even if the association is indirect.
4. Each student begins an original, creative writing related to the topic. In the *Success* program, *creative writing* is not limited to stories or poetry.
5. Ten minutes before the end of the module, call time, and ask students to proofread their papers using the proofreading thrust for that day's module, following the regular proofreading procedure.
6. Rather than filing the papers, collect them and keep them in your desk for easy distribution back to the students during the next day's Composition Module.
7. On the second day, lead a brief discussion related to the topic but direct the discussion to include ideas and information not discussed on the previous day. Write key words and phrases volunteered by the students on the chalkboard as before.
8. Papers begun on the first day are returned.
9. The students read their papers, correct any errors they note while reading, and add to the content of the first day's writing, using the ideas provided by the introductory discussion or others they choose.
10. Students proofread their papers for the proofreading thrust suggested and then exchange papers for peer-interaction proofreading.
11. When the proofreading is completed, writers date and file the papers.

EXAMPLES OF VARIOUS WRITING FORMS

Teachers and individual students are free to develop a lesson differently. The proofreading thrust and the writing mode can change even when the topic for writing remains the same. As the year progresses, most students increase the quantity and quality of their writings, but the proofreading technique continues to be incorporated each day.

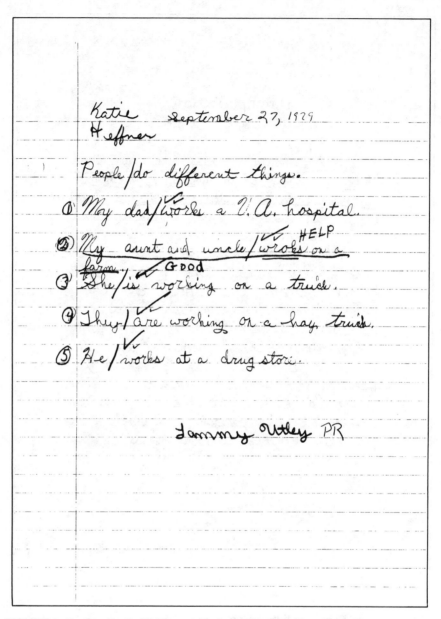

FIGURE 3–9   Student's Writing at End of a Composition Module

There is also an amazing variation in how students take the same set of directions concerning a Composition Module, and write differing styles and content about the topic.

An example (Figure 3–11) illustrates the writing of paragraphs. In Lesson 86 the students were to write a paragraph about "flying kites with friends." The proofreading thrust was to use a *possessive pronoun*.

Another type of segment writing is poetry. Fig-

ure 3–12 is a Haiku poem written during Lesson 73. Letters are a third form of segment writing, and students learn appropriate letter forms in Cycle 8.

Time-lapse writing extends the same topic for more than one day. A two-day time-lapse writing can have a different proofreading thrust for each day. This composition could start in Lesson 15 and be completed in Lesson 16 the following academic day.

Time-lapse writing can be written over a five day

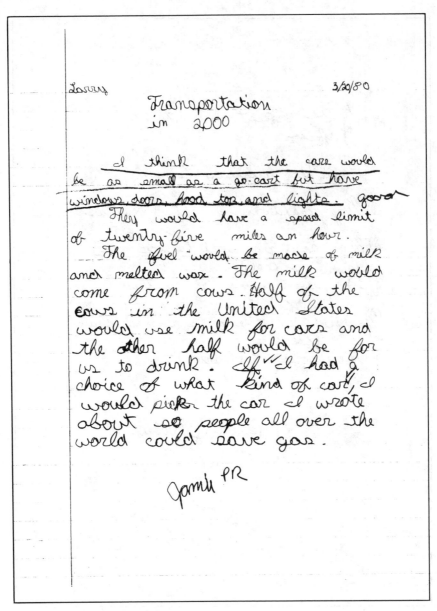

FIGURE 3–10 Segment Writing from Lesson 156

period, incorporating, for example, Lessons 131, 132, 133, 134, and 135 of the Composition Module. Each day the student is writing the story, there is a different proofreading thrust. After proofreading with a partner, the student is encouraged to make corrections before turning his or her paper in to the teacher.

PROGRESS RECORD OF STUDENT

Some students, either because they have never had many opportunities to write, they feel they have noth-

ing to say, or they have been conditioned not to like writing, are very hesitant and slow to get started at the beginning of the year.

The following student example, in Figure 3–13, is included to show how through constant, daily positive feedback from the teacher, the built-in skills in daily lessons, and the increased self-confidence of the student, a reluctant writer became an eager writer.

The student's writing improved not only in volume but in content. There are still areas for improvement but the student is now enjoying writing and as

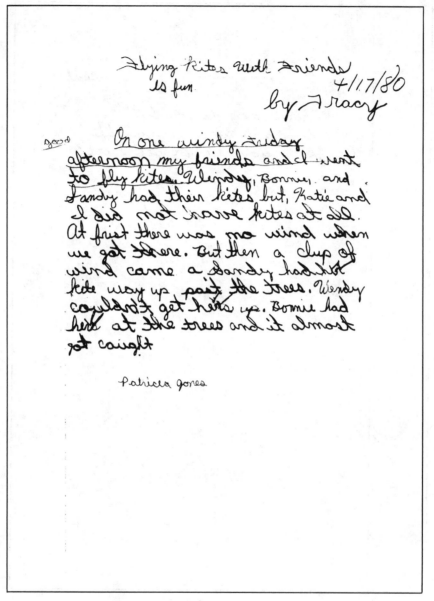

FIGURE 3–11 Lesson 86 Developed in Paragraph—Proofreading for Possessive Pronouns

he continues in school will be able to learn ways to improve his writing each year.

REWRITING

Authors write and rewrite. Students need to develop a desire not only to express themselves through the written word, but to do it in the best possible way. Writing a paper, proofreading it, correcting some errors, and filing the paper is often all that is needed to develop the desire to write.

Do not ask students to rewrite every day. However, several times during the year students should be given class time to rewrite compositions after they have been proofread. This helps the students realize that the rewriting process can be rewarding when they have a finished product that shows improvement over the original. There should be a specific reason given for rewriting such as displaying on a bulletin board,

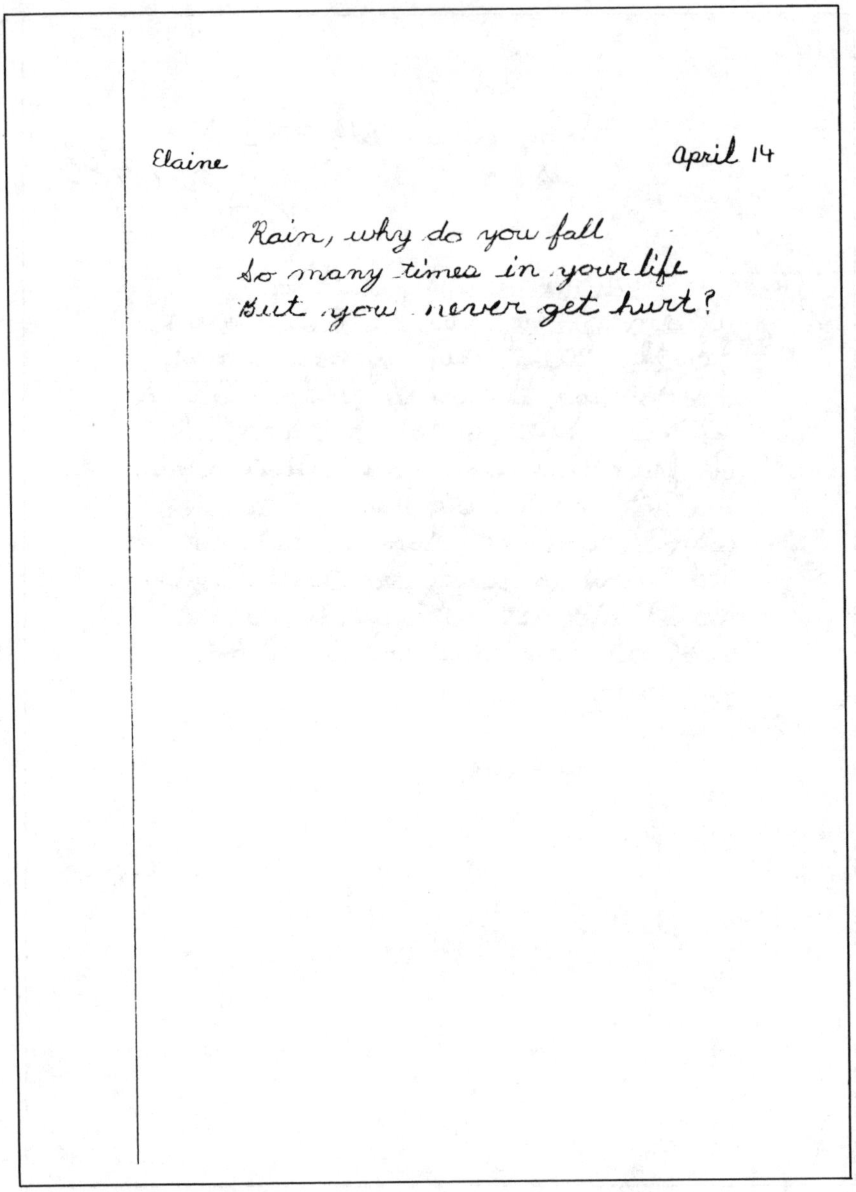

Elaine   April 14

Rain, why do you fall
So many times in your life
But you never get hurt?

FIGURE 3–12   Haiku Poetry in Lesson 73

publishing in a book, or sharing with a parent. Rewriting simply for the physical motions involved has no purpose.

PEER GROUP SHARING

Fourth-grade students are very anxious to share their compositions with each other. It is impossible to let each child read his or her composition every day. The following are suggestions for class sharing periods.

Make a point to call on one or two students each day to read their compositions orally at the end of the module.

Divide students into small groups of 3–4 to read their compositions orally to each other.

Set aside a period of time either in the mornings or afternoons for "Presenting Young Authors" when students who wish may gather in a designated place in the classroom to read and listen to compositions.

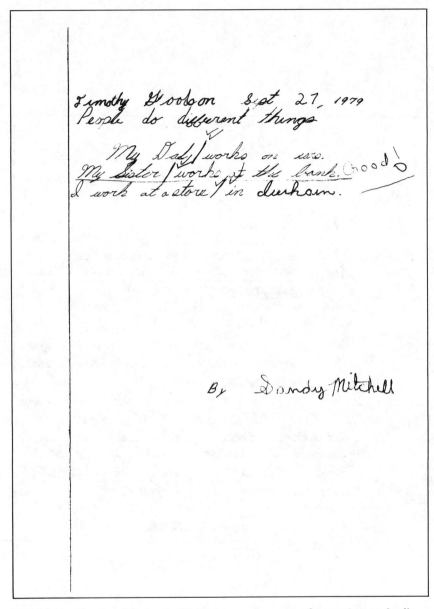

FIGURE 3–13   One Student's Writing Improvement—September to April

STENCILS AND TAPE RECORDERS

At least once a month each student should write a creative paper on a blank ditto stencil. Copies should be made available to each class member. (Most students also like to record their writing on a blank tape. Other students can listen to the tape while they read the stencil copy of the writing.) This technique allows students to learn to read handwriting of different people. Each student should take his or her copy of the writing home.

HANDWRITING IMPROVEMENT

Concern has been expressed about the letter formation, spacing, etc., of some students. There is an easy way to help students improve their handwriting. Establish the policy that each day before students hand in papers, they circle the best-formed letter on that paper. They should change the letter with each paper. For example, ask students to circle the best *s* written on one paper, the best *l* on another paper, or the best capital letter on the paper.

51

FIGURE 3–13 (continued)

Timothy G   March 17,

A story about a
kite flying contest

Last year on Saint
Patricks Day I saw two boys
in a feld with kites. I
went to get my kite. I
rode my bike to the fild.
I put my kite in the air.
The boys said whats
your name "I said Tim". The
boy said "Do you what to
have a kite flying contest". I said
yes I do." We put the
line in the fild so we
would now were to start.
The boy said go. We
ran to the kites. got in
the air. My kite went
the higest. The boy said
I won. I got my bike
and went home.

FIGURE 3–13   (continued)

1

April 18

Shipwrecked

Once upon a time
I was going fishing in the
sea. I saw a boat and it
was brown and black. I dropped
my fishing pole and jumped
on the boat. I turned the
switch on and put it in ser.
It was on May 6, 1973. I went
to see if every thing was
ready to go and it was ready to go.
I went in the botton
of the boat. I saw a man
and he was dead. I went back
in the top of the boat. I
put it in trive and trove
in the menttle of the sea.
and the boat cut off. I tried
to grake it back but it
wouldn't grake back. I went
back in the bottle to get
the C.B and to get some help.

FIGURE 3–13   (continued)

I got some help but
they didn't come. I jumped in
the water and started to swim
to shor. When I got to shor
I went to get my friend Todd.
He is 11 years old and has
brown hair. He is in forth
grade. He was in the front yard.
I said, do you want to go with me
    "yes" "Todd said" lets go.
I showed him the boat. We
jumped in the water and went to
the boat. When we got to
the boat we put the mom
on the bed. We got the
boat started. We went on
down the sea. We saw a
snake in the water and it
was a black snake. We
stop to kill it because it
it kind bit someone. The
boat got stuck in
the sand we couldn't
get it unstick because
we want strong euf.

FIGURE 3–13   (continued)

55

We got the boat
unstuck. We got back in the
boat. We take down the sea.
We saw people swimming in
the water. We turned the
E-B on and hard that two
little boys was lost in the sea.
We turned off the E-B and
put it up. We saw a nother
black snake. We stopped and I
pick it up. The snake pit me.
I had to cut my arm open
to get the person out.
We saw a house in the woods and we
was happy to see a house. We
got out of the boat and went
to get in the house. We was
so happy that we got a place to
keep warm and to sleep in
beds. It was a nice place for
children. We was so happy to
get to het the food. We went
to get the stuff out of the
boat and the boat was not
thier. I said, "did you leve the

FIGURE 3–13   (continued)

> the boat in ger "ino" I said.
> We went back in the house.
> We went to put some shorts on
> and go swimming in the sea. I
> saw the boat in the bottle of
> the sea and I went to get my
> stuff out of the boat. I got stuff
> out of the boat. I got out of
> the sea and went in the house. We
> went to get somthing to eat. We
> got two hotdogs and two trakes.
> We ate and them we saw the
> police man. He said wore is
> your mom and your daily we sad
> that we run away. He card us
> home.
>
> T
> h
> e nd
>
> By Timoth Goodson

FIGURE 3–13   (continued)

DAILY COMPOSITION INSTRUCTION

The Composition Modules are a basic framework within which you can be flexible. Themes may be substituted if another topic is of greater interest to the class than the one suggested in the module. You may wish to allow more than one day for a theme or more time for a proofreading thrust; however, the proofreading thrusts will be repeated at later times during the year. On days when longer writings are requested, such as short stories, the writing might be continued as a homework assignment.

SUMMARY

There are five major parts in each Composition Module: (1) selecting a writing theme, a writing mode, and at least one proofreading thrust; (2) prewriting discussion; (3) student writing; (4) students proofreading their own papers; and (5) each student proofreading another student's paper. The authors have researched the skills traditionally found in "compartmentalized" language lessons (writing complete sentences, subject-verb agreement, etc.) and have incorporated them in the Composition lessons. Each should be developed *during the writing process* instead of in separate, unconnected lessons such as are found on workbook pages and in language books. The emphasis should be on helping students develop accuracy in the *mechanics* of writing, while encouraging them to be specific in the *content* they write.

References

Anderson, P. S. *Language Skills in Elementary Education.* 2nd ed. New York: Macmillan, 1972.

Bolinger, Dwight. *Regarding Language.* New York: Harcourt Brace Jovanovich, 1972.

McKee P., et al. *Reading for Meaning.* Boston: Houghton Mifflin, 1966.

Smith, E. Brooks, Kenneth S. Goodman, and Robert Meredith. *Language and Thinking in the Elementary School.* New York: Holt, Rinehart and Winston, 1970.

Tiedt, Sidney W., and Iris M. Tiedt. *Language Arts Activities for the Classroom.* Boston: Allyn and Bacon, 1978. (See especially Chapter Two.)

Wolf, W., et al. *Critical Reading Ability of Elementary School Children.* Project No. 5–1040, U.S. Office of Education, 1967.

chapter four
How to Teach the Study Skills Module

RATIONALE

The third 30 minutes of each lesson emphasize one of the most important aspects of reading and writing—effective study skills. Rather than identify study skills and create "mock" materials for students to read as they apply the skills, the *Success* Study Skills Modules:

1. identify a specific study skill;
2. suggest a reading assigment where students use the study skill as they read content area textbooks, newspapers, and other materials;
3. correlate the reading assignment with a writing assignment; and
4. provide a thematic format that can extend for several days.

Objectives of the Study Skills Module include providing opportunities for students to think, read, and write about their findings to the extent they can explain information gained. Comparisons with the findings and thoughts of others in the class are encouraged during the last part of the module, after a quiet time has been provided in class for students to study.

Some students believe "learning" comes only from academic textbooks. By coordinating study skills with a variety of printed information, students realize that although important, the academic textbook is only one source of information.

Although the Study Skills Module emphasizes academic content in textbooks and other reference materials, it also correlates the process of locating information and other study techniques with an assortment of printed materials available in a person's life usually outside of school. Figure 4–1 is an example of this correlation. The paper was developed during Lesson 79 and the students used menus to locate specific information. Refer to the Study Skills Module in Lesson 79 for the specific assignment given to the students during this module.

To illustrate the inclusion of more academic-type printed material in many of the Study Skills Modules, Figure 4–2 shows a student's paper developed during Lesson 48. Class members used either an encyclopedia or a social studies textbook and each student located a land map (part one of the assignment); found the map key or legend (part two of the assignment); selected information to write (part three of the assignment); wrote major facts located (part four of the assignment); and, if time permitted, drew the map. This particular student elected to put information found in two columns. Other students in the class wrote information in sentences, in charts, etc. *All* learned to find at least one fact in a land map and relate the fact to the map. Some students wrote more than others, depending on their abilities and interests.

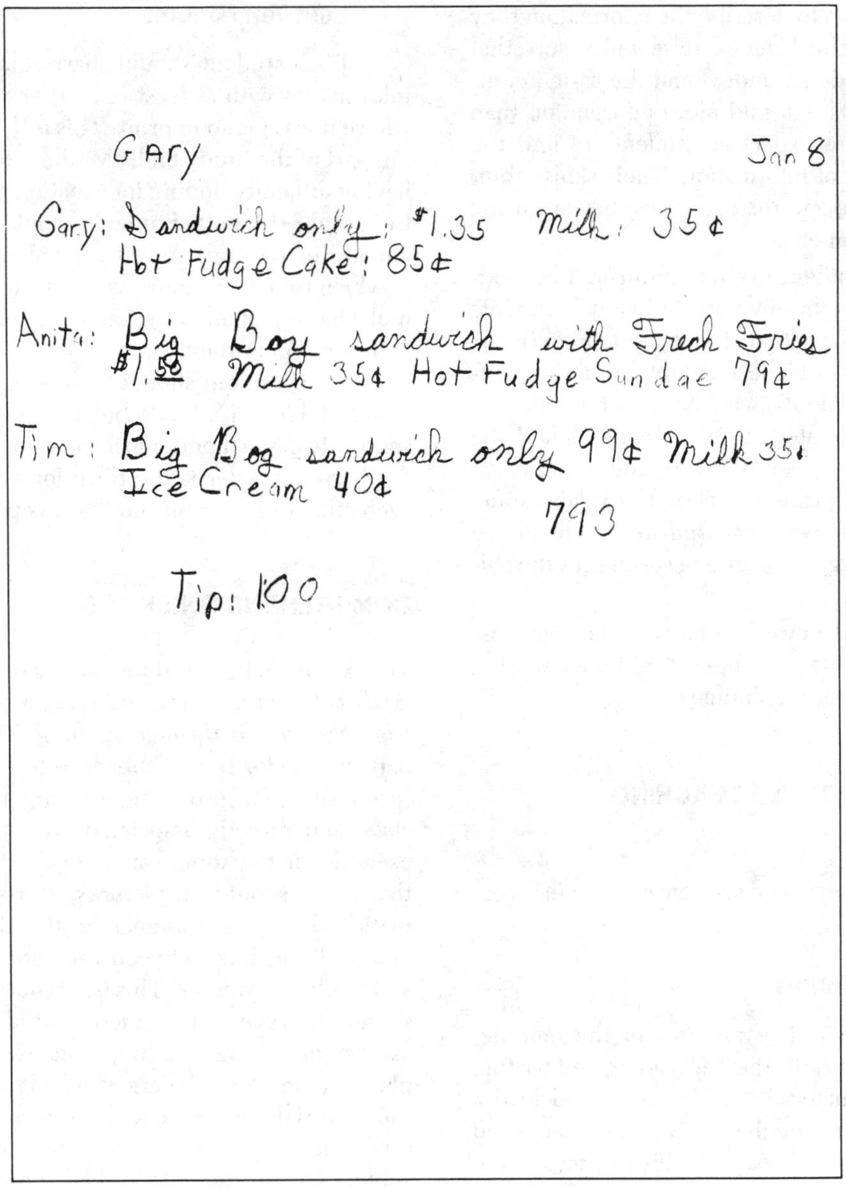

GARY   Jan 8

Gary: Sandwich only: $1.35   Milk: 35¢
Hot Fudge Cake: 85¢

Anita: Big Boy sandwich with French Fries
$1.50 Milk 35¢ Hot Fudge Sundae 79¢

Tim: Big Boy sandwich only 99¢ Milk 35¢
Ice Cream 40¢
                                   793

        Tip: 100

FIGURE 4–1   Student's Paper from Lesson 79—Study Skills Module

Teaching the Study Skills Module incorporates a markedly different approach from that of handing out a workbook page with a predetermined number of blank spaces to be filled in by zeroing in on the thought processes of the person who developed the page. It differs also from using a textbook chapter with accompanying questions at the end. During the first part of the Study Skills Module, each student locates the information he or she can during the allocated time. Then, time is provided for students to share some of the information found with other members of the class.

Since this module is open-ended, the following three points are extremely important in helping the teacher avoid frustration, especially at the beginning of the year.

1. In a preliminary discussion when the assignment is introduced, locate something related to the assignment. Discuss its relationship. Allow one

or two students to describe the information they have found. This brief exercise will ensure that almost all students understand the assignment. Some students will find more information than others. Do not expect all students to find the same amount of information. Their skills, abilities, interests, and the resources they are using are not the same.

2. Move from student to student during this module conversing briefly with individual students about the information they have found. Incorporate the comprehension emphasis in your conversation. Students who have not found any information related to the topic should be assisted in doing so by the teacher. Locate an item in the printed material, explain some aspect of it briefly *to that student* (not the entire class), and suggest something specific for the student to write.

3. Allow students to work in pairs or small groups. This will provide more opportunities for sharing ideas and defending findings.

STUDY SKILLS MODULE TEACHING SEQUENCE

The following is a suggested sequence to use in teaching this module.

First Five Minutes

During the first five minutes in the module, introduce the study skill, theme, reading and writing assignments, the material(s) to be used, and lead a discussion concerning the theme. Note the theme and assignments on the chalkboard. Your directions to the class should be very short and very specific. Many students can begin work immediately and should not have to wait through several explanations of the assignment.

Next Fifteen Minutes

Students begin immediately to read silently, with no talking to other students during this part of the module. Students should write as they find information, not wait until after they have finished reading the entire selections. You should move from student to student, helping as many as possible on an individual basis. Each student writes his or her name and the date at the top of the page.

Last Ten Minutes

Each student should share some of the written information with at least one other student and note where it was found in print. This is the internal grouping part of the Study Skills Module. Students who are having difficulty finding information may receive help from other students. Students should select their own partner or partners unless they abuse the privilege, at which time you should assign group members. This oral sharing of information with another person is extremely important.

Each student should file the paper in his or her manila folder in a box labeled *Study Skills*. Do not send this paper home until the end of the year. The Study Skills folder is the third longitudinal record of each student's work in the *Success* program.

COMPREHENSION SKILLS

The Study Skills Module endorses the concepts of (1) *direct* (literal) and (2) *indirect* (interpretive) *knowledge association through reading*. Traditionally, the pattern was for the teacher to select a theme and be responsible for providing reading materials in the classroom directly associated with that theme. For example, if the topic was animals, the thought was that there should be pictures, stories, factual information, etc., about animals in the classroom to provide a direct link between the subject of the lesson and reading materials. This is, of course, educationally sound; however, the practice of direct knowledge association through reading when used exclusively has placed a drain on teachers who feel *they* must compile the materials. Unfortunately, topics sometimes have not been introduced because "there is nothing on the subject for the students to read about."

The Study Skills Module does not restrict reading to direct association. The students are taught, also, how to relate a topic to a specific category through an indirect thinking process. For example, if the module subtheme is *animals*, it is conceivable that a student would find the word, a description, or a picture of *carrots* and associate carrots with *rabbits*. The process of indirect association bridges the gap between the obvious (the word *horse*) and the relationship of a description of a *pasture* to horses. Most important, the student is responsible for the thinking process. No subtheme in the Study Skills Module should be delayed because "there are no materials on that topic in the classroom." Students have a tremendous imag-

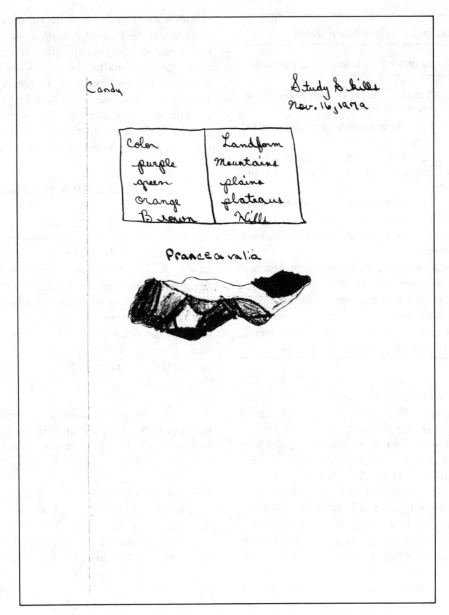

FIGURE 4–2 Student's Paper from Lesson 48—Study Skills Module

ination and ability to perform indirect associations in class, if provided opportunities. Having a wide variety of printed materials in the room is essential, however.

Making direct and indirect reading/knowledge association is an extremely important research skill and should be introduced as early as possible in the academic year. One of the most striking features of this approach is the relief it brings to teachers who no longer have to delay a topic until *they* have done the physical work of locating related information. Instead,

the students are involved in the process of association of printed information with specific topics.

COMPREHENSION QUESTIONS

You should ask comprehension questions on an individual basis at the student's desk after you have glanced at the information he or she is reading.

To help students in comprehending the infor-

63

TABLE 4–1 Internal Comprehension Guide

Cycle Day	Comprehension Question Emphasis
Day 1	Ask student to locate *who* and *what* information related to the theme
Day 2	Ask student to locate *why* information related to the theme
Day 3	Ask student to locate information that he or she considers *most important* about the theme
Day 4	Ask student to locate *where* and *when* information related to the theme
Day 5	Ask student to locate *any information* related to the theme
Day 6	Ask student to locate information *not related* to the theme, and to explain reasons
Day 7	Ask student to locate *specific, factual details* about the theme
Day 8	Ask students to make *interpretations* based on information read about the theme

---

mation they find that relates to a topic, Table 4–1 offers a comprehension focus guide for use in the Study Skills Module. This guide provides a minimal structure that will ensure that all types of comprehension questions are focused on regularly. Do not feel limited to asking only questions using the day's comprehension emphasis. More than likely, it will be appropriate to ask questions based on several additional emphases during each Study Skills Module. You should ask such questions during the whole class discussion of the theme, when directing the students in their reading and writing assignments, and when walking around the room while they are reading and writing. In order to answer the question, the student may be required to read a passage from his or her material or defend a statement written on his or her paper.

Many students are spending countless hours in fragmentary reading combined with "checks of reading and/or writing skills." There is reason to believe that these checks, such as questions at the end of a paragraph or chapter, and fill-in-the-blank type sentences, may *not* in actuality reveal information about the student's reading/writing abilities. For example, in a so-called comprehension check labeled "Ability to Detect Main Ideas," the student may write an incorrect response *because the main ideas the student perceived were different from those the writer of the question perceived*. Two injustices have been accomplished: (1) the student's reading comprehension abilities were not recognized; and (2) the student was penalized for not thinking along the same lines as another person. Constant exposure to this type of reading exercise creates "fractured" reading and discourages reading an entire selection for information or simply for pleasure. Some students, unfortunately, become masters of the system but hate to read.

RESEARCH AND STUDY TECHNIQUES

Some of the Study Skills Module cycles emphasize various research techniques and other cycles emphasize various study techniques. Cycle 4, Lessons 24–30, *Making Charts and Tables* is an example of a research technique. In Lesson 29, students locate automobile information in the classified advertisements of a newspaper and develop a chart showing some of the information found. Figure 4–3 shows a student's paper written during that lesson in a fourth-grade class. There are errors on the paper, however the student has shown he can perform this type of research.

Near the end of some of the Study Skills cycles, you may wish to use the chalkboard and create a class summary of information students located during the earlier part of the module. Using Lesson 29 again as an example, Figure 4–4 is a copy of a chart a teacher wrote on the chalkboard to include some of the information the students found. The students volunteered the content of the chart. The student whose work appears in Figure 4–3 volunteered "Pinto"; another student had a different price for the car. Such sessions are usually lively. If this approach is used, it should be after the students have written some of the information they gathered while reading.

As one gathers information, the ability to classify content is an extremely important study skill. Taking notes along with the classification is encompassed in Cycle 15, *Classification*, Lessons 80–82. To illustrate how one student completed this study skills technique, see Figure 4–5, a student's paper developed during Lesson 81. The student selected key words from the sports section of a newspaper and was asked to divide those words into any two categories of her choosing. She selected the categories of *nouns* and *verbs*. This paper illustrates that study skills lessons can be taught with printed materials other than traditional academic textbooks.

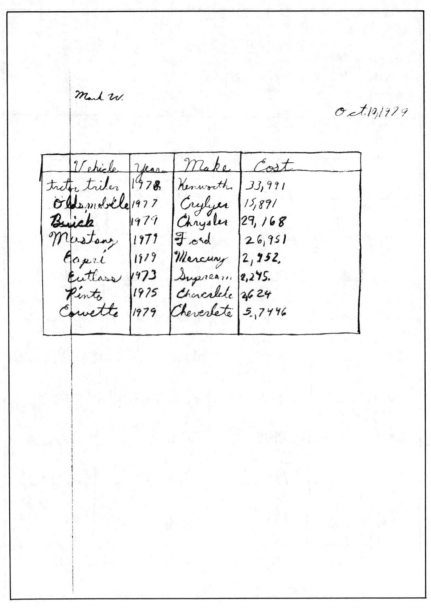

FIGURE 4–3   Student's Chart Developed During Lesson 29—Newspaper Research

THE CYCLES

Throughout the academic year, important study skills are introduced in cycles. For example, one cycle emphasizes locating factual information and taking notes on facts; another cycle stresses reading maps and writing information found on the maps. You should look at the third column in the lessons in Appendix One and note that more days are suggested for some

Lesson - 29
Material - Classified Ads / Newspapers
Emphasis

Vehicle	Year	Make	Cost
truck	1975	Ford	$15,000.⁰⁰
car	1973	Ford Pinto	$895.⁰⁰
truck	1972	Ford	$1,695.⁰⁰
car	1977	Buick Lasabre	$3,950.⁰⁰
motorcycle	1980	Harley Davidson	no price stated
car	1977	Regal - Buick	$121.⁰⁰ per month
car	1979	Caprice Wagon - Chev	$7,348.⁰⁰
car	1949	Ford	$4,450.⁰⁰
car	1977	Ford	$2,287.⁰⁰
truck	1977	Ford	$3,295.⁰⁰
car	1969	Firebird - Pontiac	$1,295.⁰⁰

FIGURE 4–4   Class Chart Developed During Lesson 29

cycles than for others, depending on the frequency with which students need to use a particular study skill.

Lessons 1–60 emphasize different study skills as they relate to content areas. Beginning with Lesson 61, on the recommendation of teachers in a pilot program, the emphasis is reversed, with the content topic stressed and an associated study skill included, also.

This module provides a comprehensive framework for the teacher to use in teaching study skills. If the class is a remedial reading class, some of the cycles may need to be extended over a greater number of days. On the other hand, advanced students may not need as many days for a particular cycle. Teacher expertise should determine how long each cycle should be taught in a particular class.

Table 4–2 lists the various study skills as they are emphasized in cycles, and the lesson numbers for each cycle. This list should be helpful to you in planning.

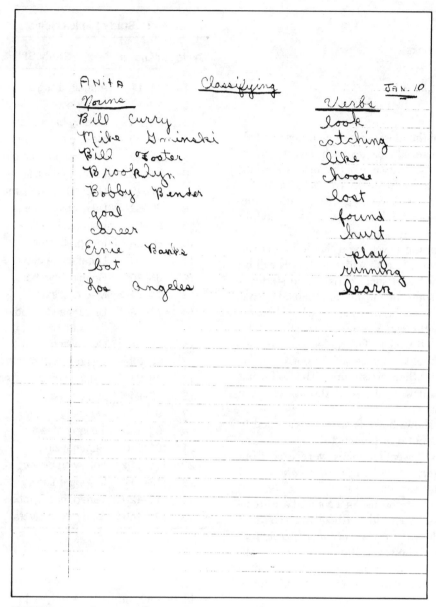

FIGURE 4–5   Student's Paper from Lesson 81—Classification Study Skill

During the latter part of the academic year, a variety of study skills is introduced in an overlapping fashion. Table 4–3 is a partial list of the kinds of study skills emphasized to illustrate the diversity of foci.

THE MATERIALS

Each study skill is taught in conjunction with a variety of printed materials. The following lists only a few of the many resources suggested in the Study Skills Module:

science textbooks
social studies textbooks
newspapers
health textbooks
magazines
music textbooks

67

encyclopedias
dictionaries
mathematics textbooks
fiction books
maps
travel brochures

This is one of the most difficult modules to introduce, since the material changes each day; however, later in the year, it becomes one of the most rewarding for both teacher and students. To compensate for changing materials and reading/writing directions each day, the procedural format for this module remains the same for the academic year.

Before beginning a cycle, you should look at the Study Skills Module and note which materials will be needed for the cycle. In some classes, the students brought to class some of the materials needed and some came from the materials center or school library. Teachers used mathematics, science, social studies, health, and music textbooks for grades two through nine, found in school storage closets or borrowed for short terms from other classrooms. The following examples of student work illustrate the use of three different materials.

Figure 4–6 shows how magazines were used to teach *multiple meanings* in Lesson 131.

In Figure 4–7 weather maps were used from newspapers to *interpret and graph information*. This example is from Lesson 126.

Figure 4–8 illustrates use of a content area textbook. Lesson 130 uses a health textbook to teach *cause and effect*. This lesson suggests *accident prevention* as the topic for focus; however, the teacher was teaching a dental health unit and made an adjustment in the lesson to correlate it with the current topic under study.

An objective of this module is to teach students techniques that will enable them to locate information independently, or to note quickly that the information sought is not found in a particular source, thus necessitating their looking in a different source. In actuality, when a person needs information on a topic, no one is around to tell that person which book, page number, and paragraph contains the information. Students may have, although it is not necessary, the same edition of a book or other material during this module; however, for the reason stated above, a variety of materials may be more useful.

Students can write papers based on information

read in encyclopedias such as in Lesson 54 in the Study Skills Module. Probably, no two students in the classroom will find and/or record the same information or use the same encyclopedia pages.

CORRELATION WITH CONTENT AREA INSTRUCTION

A long-established and accepted part of the upper elementary curriculum is instruction in subjects such as mathematics, social studies, science, and health. The Study Skills Module is not intended to replace any content area lesson; however, the modules are

TABLE 4–2 Study Skills Cycles

Cycle	Lessons	Study Skill Emphases
1	1–11	Alphabetizing
2	12–17	Sequence
3	18–23	Finding basic facts
4	24–30	Making charts and tables
5	31–40	Information from pictures
6	41–46	Locating specific words
7	47–49	Understanding a map key
8	50–52	Developing listening skills
9	53–55	Using a time line
10	56–58	Interpreting graphs
11	59–64	Locating details
12	65–70	Reading symbols
13	71–73	Map reading
14	74–78	Understanding advertised information
15	79–82	Classifying
16	83–88	Using a card catalogue
17	89–91	Using correct reference sources
18	92–94	Main ideas
19	95–97	Outlining
20	98–100	Taking notes
21	101–110	Summarizing
22	111–114	Following directions
23	115–117	Making a survey
24	118–120	Varied map symbols
25	121–180	Study skills diversity

TABLE 4–3   Selected Examples of Study Skills in "Study Skills Diversity," Lessons 121–180

Lessons	Study Skill	Lessons	Study Skill
121	Observing and reporting	138	Recognizing story settings
122	Completing order forms	139, 142	Recognizing sensory
122, 125	Making judgments		imagery
123, 127, 144	Locating main ideas	140	Following directions
123, 137, 146, 153, 160, and 164	Locating and recalling details	141, 145, 156, 161, 168, 171, 176, and 180	Relating information
124, 143, 177	Making comparisons	162, 178	Making analogies/
124	Using reference materials		associations
126, 133, 140, 146, 154,		148, 167	Making inferences
162, and 170	Using map skills	149, 173	Recognizing author's
126, 174	Graphing information		intent
127	Using diagrams for	150, 165, 166, 170	Detecting symbolism
	information	151	Recognizing similes and
127, 160	Determining sequence		metaphors
128, 152	Summarizing	155, 163	Defining words in context
129	Understanding fact and	157	Forming conclusions
	opinion	158	Detecting techniques of
130, 135	Noting causes and effects		persuasion
131	Noting multiple meanings	164	Using index
132	Using glossary	172	Recognizing satire
132, 147	Using key words as clues to main ideas	175	Selecting information from charts
134, 159	Making predictions	179	Classifying information
136	Using abbreviations	179	Alphabetizing

intended to reinforce and supplement instruction by including a specific study skill with a content area topic. You may want to change some of the suggested topics in the Study Skills Module and use others currently being studied in history, mathematics, etc. On the other hand, topics are available in each module, if you wish to use them.

The Study Skills Module adapts easily to topics you include in the base curriculum of any content area. For example, in a Study Skills cycle on teaching graphs, you might use a graph in the mathematics textbook, a stencil copy of a graph, or a graph from a magazine.

Now the correlation of various content areas in the Study Skills Module will be explained, including some student writing examples.

Academic textbooks are used frequently as the printed reference in the Study Skills Module. Instead of asking students to turn to a certain page in a certain textbook and read to locate information, the teacher of the *Success* Study Skills Modules should present a global knowledge area and ask students to use the books to find information they can associate with that theme.

Health

Figure 4–9 is a student's paper developed during the Study Skills Module in Lesson 61. Various textbooks were used in the class. This student has demonstrated she can locate information related to

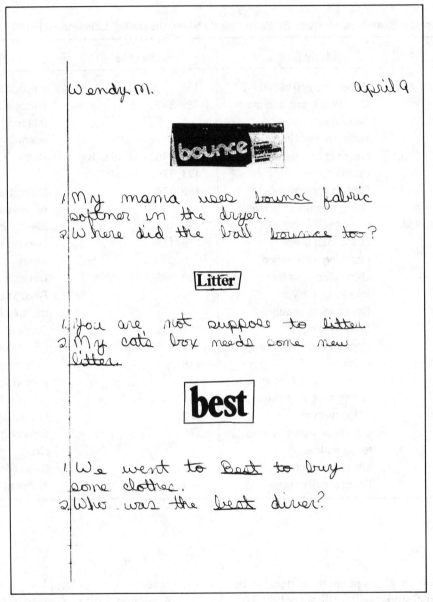

FIGURE 4–6 Student's Paper from Lesson 131—Identifying Multiple Meanings Using Magazines

health (she selected *foods* as a topic) and relate the topic to her own health.

Often at the upper elementary level teachers feel pressed for time to teach each subject they are responsible for teaching. Integration of knowledge areas is found within the Study Skills Module. You may wish to change a module, substituting a content area lesson that deals with a specific study skill and provides extra exposure to the material being covered in the unit under study.

Figures 4–10 and 4–11 show how one fourth-grade teacher used the Study Skills Module to help students learn the health vocabulary for a unit she was teaching. Instead of giving each student in the classroom the same list of words, she instructed them to read the designated material and to write *words or terms they felt they needed to learn*. Students were making a decision about their needs. They were also

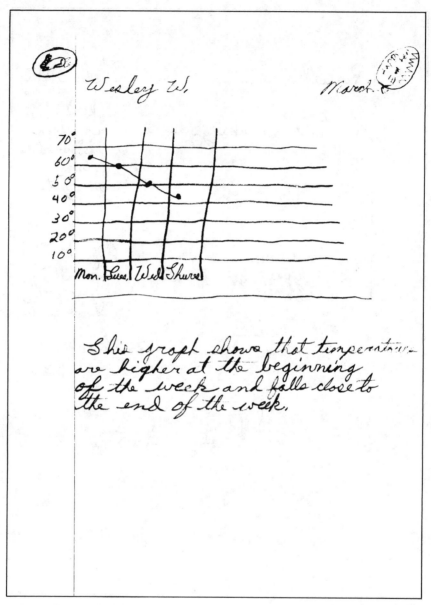

FIGURE 4–7   Student's Paper from Lesson 126—Graph Interpretation Using Newspapers

learning vocabulary needed to help them understand the material being covered.

Social Studies

Another example, Figure 4–12, shows how teachers use the Study Skills Modules with content areas taken from a social studies unit. The students read social studies textbook materials and wrote ques-tions about the information they read. They then exchanged papers with a partner who wrote the answers.

There are a variety of reading and writing assign-ments using academic textbooks in the Study Skills Module. The object is not only to illustrate to students that there are different ways of locating information in textbooks, but also that there are many different ways to record their findings.

71

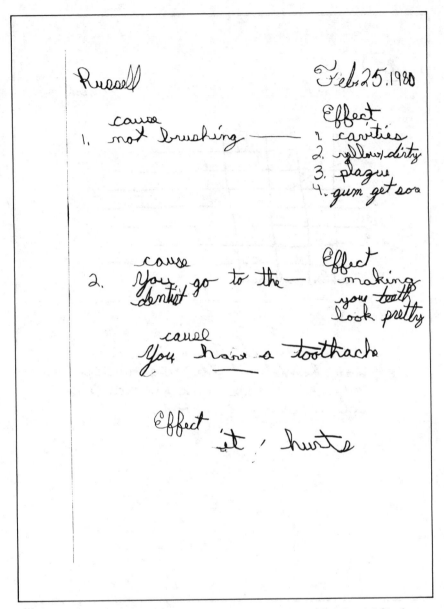

FIGURE 4–8 Student's Paper from Lesson 130—Modification of Study Topic Using Health Textbooks

Figure 4–13 is a class chart from Lesson 28 of the Study Skills Module where the printed materials are social studies textbooks. The reading theme is transportation, another traditional unit for fourth graders. Instead of reporting in sentences, the students developed charts. Refer to Lesson 28 for the specific reading and writing assignments in this module. The class chart was developed at the end of the module, as different students volunteered items from their papers at their desks, and an ongoing discussion was held between teacher and students.

Mathematics

"They have trouble *reading* their mathematics textbook" is one of the fairly common concerns expressed by fourth-grade teachers. Throughout the Study Skills Module during the academic year, the

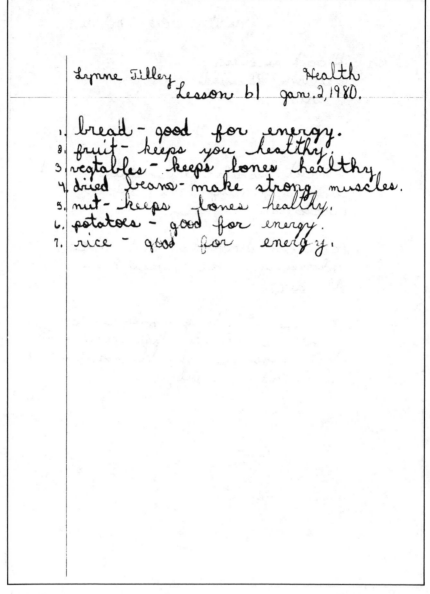

FIGURE 4–9 Student's Paper Developed While Using Health Textbook During Lesson 61

mathematics textbook is specified as the source of printed material for students to read. In addition, in the modules, other printed materials (maps, social studies textbooks, etc.) are used for students to read to locate mathematics information.

These modules are not intended, as such, to teach mathematics; rather, the object is to help students improve their reading of mathematics. However, the teacher can easily incorporate the theme of the mathematics lesson for the day with the reading/writing assignment in a Study Skills Module.

Figure 4–14 is an example of student work completed during Lesson 65. The emphasis is on the students *locating and writing symbols* and the word(s) that denote the meaning of the symbols. Note that the students may not select symbols in the same order and they may select the same as well as different mathematics symbols. You can add any base symbols that

73

april 10, 1980   Mark

Blood vessles
Carbon Dioxide
Mucus

1. Blood vessels- any tube in the body through the blood circlates.

2. carbon dioxide - colorless, odorless gas present in the air.

3. mucus - a slimy substance that is made by and that moistens the linings of body cavitys.

FIGURE 4–10   Student A's Vocabulary List from Health Textbook

you want the students to learn in addition to those symbols selected by the students.

Science

There are many specialized words in science textbooks, plus much information disseminated in a small number of words. The ability to locate information related to a particular study topic and condense the information in a way that is meaningful to the student is extremely important. Students can copy scientific information and still not understand what they are writing.

Figure 4–15 is a student's paper developed during Lesson 127. The material is a science textbook and the knowledge area is *planets*. The reading/writing assignment is for the student to look through the science textbook and either draw a diagram about planets or write information he or she associates with planets. This student chose to write rather than draw a diagram. No two students during the module wrote the same information; yet, all wrote something they could

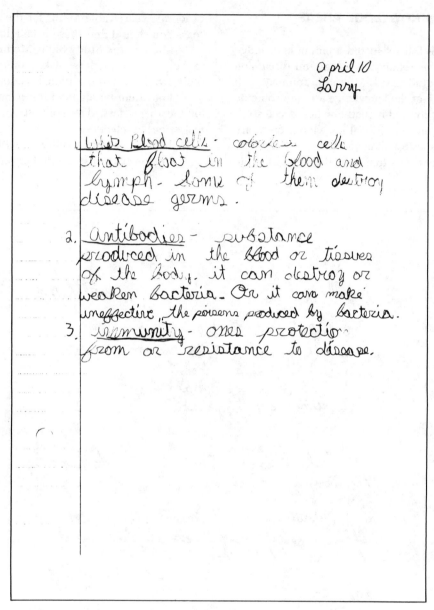

April 10
Larry

1. White Blood cells - colorless cells that float in the blood and lymph - some of them destroy disease germs.

2. Antibodies - substance produced in the blood or tissues of the body. it can destroy or weaken bacteria. Or it can make ineffective, the poisons produced by bacteria.

3. Immunity - ones protection from or resistance to disease.

FIGURE 4–11 Student B's Vocabulary List from Health Textbook

associate with the topic. The association sprang from looking through and reading information in the science textbook. It was, for the students, a meaningful exercise.

Magazines

Content area information can be found using magazines, and many of the Study Skills Modules cor-

relate academic information with popular magazine content. Frequently, the combination produces both traditional words and words found in the advertising world.

Figure 4–16 is an example of a student's paper developed during Lesson 43 where the topic of *parts of the body* associated with magazine advertisements produced the traditional *hands* and the not-so-traditional word *Ivory*.

STUDY SKILLS KNOWLEDGE AREAS

Tables 4–4 and 4–5 list selected topics of knowledge areas suggested for reading, writing, and discussion emphases in the Study Skills Modules. You may wish to substitute some of the knowledge areas to coincide with topics being studied in mathematics, social studies, science, art, etc. Additional knowledge areas are found in the Phonics/Spelling and Composition chapters. Table 4–4 contains topics for the first half of an academic year; Table 4–5 is for the remainder of the year. You should find these lists helpful in planning.

Many of the Study Skills Modules are intended to help fourth graders make connections between their own lives and traditional academic study topics.

For example, *inventions* is a long-standing topic for fourth graders. The student could look through *magazines* to select items that have been invented and write how life might be different without them.

Lesson 62 has students locating detailed infor-

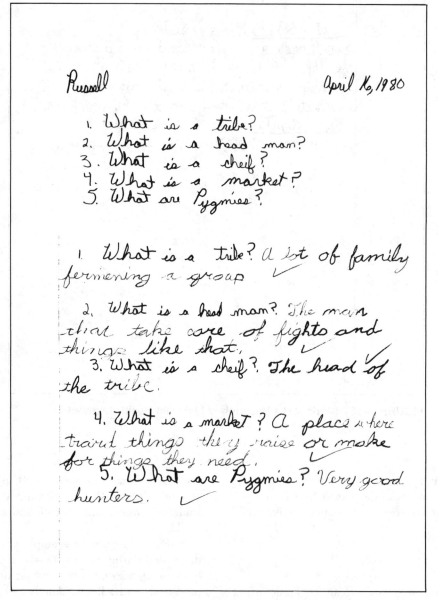

FIGURE 4–12   Student C's Questions and Answers from Social Studies Text-book Information

mation about inventions. You may wish to rearrange the schedule (for example, teach Lesson 64 before Lesson 62 in this module). Each module does emphasize an important study skill, but there is nothing mandatory about the sequence.

THE FIRST WEEKS OF SCHOOL

At the beginning of the year, some students will have difficulty finding information, especially since you will not do the locating for them by giving them specific page numbers, subheadings, and so on. Praise the student on *any* information found that he or she can associate, directly or indirectly, with the topic, and on anything that is written that can be defended by the student as associated with the topic.

Help students, on an individual basis at their desks, to look through the material until an item is found that can be associated with the theme. You can then briefly explain a relationship and designate some-

Lesson 28
Materials – Social Studies Book,
Emphasis Traveling

Who	When	Where	How
pioneers	long. ago	West	covered wagons
Jiro; Uncle Koso	Early the next morning	north farmland	airplane
Jasim		Nefta	camel caravan
Columbus	1492	India/New World	Ship
Eskimos Arluk-Nik	winter	Baffin Island Home	Dog Sled
Tito	Before daylight	fair	llamas

FIGURE 4–13   Class Chart Developed During Lesson 28—Information from Social Studies Textbooks

77

thing for the student to read and write before moving on to help another student. Then each time that you work with that student, ask him or her to locate something in print and explain it in conjunction with the theme.

Figure 4–17 illustrates this procedure. During Lesson 31, in the Study Skills Module, each student uses magazine pictures and story content to locate information about the topic *people at work*. As you move around the room, stop at each desk briefly. If the student is still turning pages, find a picture in the magazine and in two or three sentences discuss how that picture might relate to "people at work," and suggest that the student begin writing some of the infor-

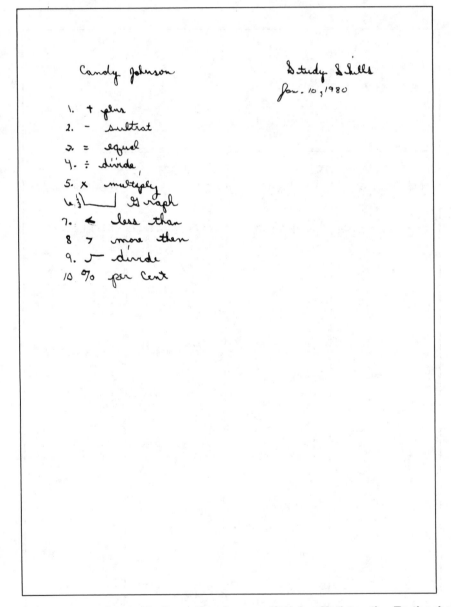

FIGURE 4–14   Student's Paper from Lesson 65 Using Mathematics Textbooks

mation discussed. With students who are already in the process of reading or writing, who understand the assignment and are underway completing it, ask what they are doing and one way it relates to the theme of the lesson before moving to the next student.

For Figure 4–17, the student was still turning pages when the teacher pointed to a picture on an open page in the magazine, and the picture was included in an article about Venezuela. With only a brief discussion about the people working with the *coffee beans* (which was the subject of one of the pictures), that student was ready to write the first entry on her page. The remainder of the page was developed by the student without input from the teacher. Since

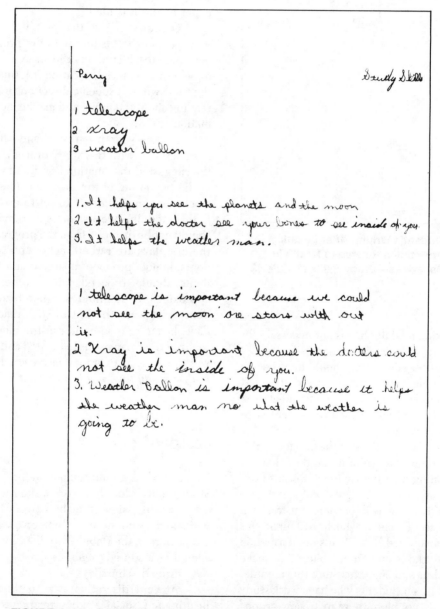

FIGURE 4–15   Student's Paper from Lesson 127 Using Science Textbooks

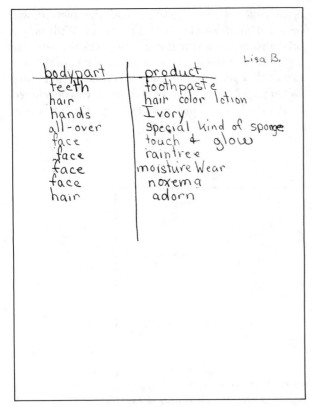

bodypart	product
teeth	toothpaste
hair	hair color lotion
hands	Ivory
all-over	special kind of sponge
face	touch & glow
face	raintree
face	moisture Wear
face	noxema
hair	adorn

Lisa B.

FIGURE 4–16   Student's Writing After Locating Information Related to Health in Magazines—Study Skills Module 43

this was a notetaking module, it was not necessary for the student to write complete sentences.

The basic process described should be used, no matter what the subject of the magazine picture is. At the end of this module, all students had found at least one way to associate magazine picture content with the topic "people at work."

Even during the first days of the program, this module can be a delight to teach if you do not stress each student locating a particular item. Because different materials are used, students will not locate identical information and will become frustrated if instructed to do so. Teachers who have taught this module have been amazed at the kinds of information found by their students and their abilities to make relationships. Relax, and enjoy teaching this module.

Do not give up on students who have weak study skills. Above all, do not place them in a "slow-group"

separate from their peers. The student who locates one word or picture and can relate that to the theme has taken the first step toward independent studying.

During the first few days of this program, some students will spend the time reading to locate information and will not have time to write anything. Their paper should be dated and filed with the notation, "Reading—no writing." You should give them credit for the reading part of the module, and make a comment orally to the effect, "Maybe soon you'll not only read, but also have time to write something on your paper before it is filed."

Quantity is not the purpose of this module, especially at the beginning of the program. The purpose is to teach students the study skill of selecting a topic and a material, locating information related to the topic without specific directions from the teacher, reading about the topic, and making notes of key information found.

As the year progresses and students become more familiar with this study process, they will locate the suggested information faster and write more than at the beginning of the program. It will take several weeks for some students to start becoming proficient in this module. Because of its extreme importance, it should not be dropped from the program, even though the first days are rather hectic, and some of the students do not "produce" a large quantity of work. Students should proceed into another module after approximately 30 minutes. Some teachers found students who were the last to start reading for several days, began to read earlier in the module when they realized their paper was to be filed and their time limit was the same as everyone else each day. *Learning to budget study time is a key element in this program.*

HOMEWORK

Homework assignments found in the Composition and Study Skills Modules are considered optional. You may wish to assign other homework topics or homework on days not noted for homework in the modules. Homework in the Phonics/Spelling Module, however, should be assigned each school night, especially Mondays through Thursdays.

At your discretion, use mathematics, science, health, and social studies textbooks for homework

TABLE 4–4 Selected Knowledge Areas in the Study Skills Module, First Half of Academic Year, Lessons 1–90

names of people	dwellings	machines	measurement
food products	comparative buying	transportation	presidents
ownership	products	politicians	money
activities at home	towns and cities	plants	automobiles
television	characters in books	economy	book titles
science projects	recipes	famous people	book topics
title pages	national parks and recreational facilities	television personalities	authors
		story settings	letter symbols
advertisements	family	autobiographies	punctuation symbols
motor vehicles	mileage charts	sports	math symbols
scientists	historical events	construction materials	real estate
labels	travel	food	card catalogue
land forms	occupations	inventions	buying and selling
graphs	parts of the body	states	

TABLE 4–5 Selected Knowledge Areas in the Study Skills Module, Second Half of Academic Year, Lessons 91–180

sea animals	bees	blood	computers
grids	money	cities	charts
graphs	emergencies	reptiles	consumerism
rainfall maps	meteors	directions	hair
frogs	nutrition	holidays	help wanted advertise-ments
conservation	fables	rivers	
planets	famous people	seasons	railroads
accident prevention	animals		physical fitness
brain	foreign country	poetry	mountains
earthquakes	television guides	amphibians	symbolism
city maps	abbreviations	sports	parks
pollution	products	current events	satires
present, past, future story settings	area codes	population maps	insects
		camping	recipes
weather	first aid	population	
outdoor scenes	bacteria	oceans	
comic strips	time zones	historical events	

assignments related to the topic studied during the Study Skills Module. Assign appropriate pages in these textbooks.

Spiral notebooks, rather than loose sheets of paper, are recommended for students to use when writing their homework. Each assignment should be dated and parents should sign the homework before the student brings the spiral notebook back to school.

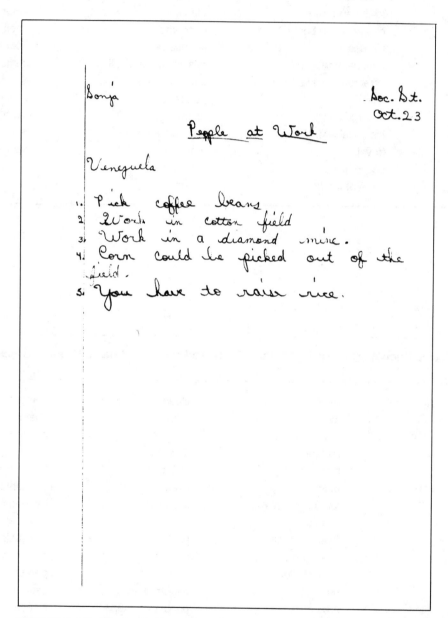

FIGURE 4–17   Student's Paper from Lesson 31—Notetaking from Magazines

References

Adams, Anne H., Charles Coble, and Paul Hounshell. *Mainstreaming Language Arts and Social Studies.* Santa Monica: Goodyear, 1977.

Coble, Charles, Paul Hounshell, and Anne H. Adams. *Mainstreaming Science and Mathematics.* Santa Monica: Goodyear, 1977.

Herber, Harold. *Teaching Reading in the Content Areas.* Englewood Cliffs, N.J.: Prentice-Hall, 1970.

Joyce, W. W., et al., eds. *Elementary Education in the Seventies.* New York: Holt, Rinehart and Winston, 1970.

Robinson, H. Alan. *Teaching Reading and Study Strategies: The Content Areas.* Boston: Allyn and Bacon, 1975.

Spache, George D. and Paul C. Berg. *The Art of Efficient Reading.* 2nd ed. New York: Macmillan, 1966.

chapter five

How to Teach the Recreational Reading Module

The fourth 30 minutes of each lesson are devoted to uninterrupted, unrestricted silent reading from a variety of fiction and nonfiction library books. The Recreational Reading Modules are found in the fourth column of each lesson in Appendix One.

RATIONALE

Children in most homes are distracted from spending extended time reading books by an amazing variety of activities. Chores, friends, the television, the telephone, and hobbies are only a few. There is little indication that this will decrease. It is essential that students have the opportunity to read books at least 30 minutes a day *during school time*. Indirectly, they learn science, history, geography, character analysis, value judgments, and much more while reading hundreds of books. This module can make one of the most significant changes in today's education, with far-reaching positive implications for the future.

The habit of reading complete novels and other books filled with information probably will not develop unless time for unassigned, sustained reading of library books for pleasure is included regularly in the instructional program. In some elementary classrooms, students go to the library and each checks out at least one book. The class returns to the classroom and the teacher says, "Put your library book in your desk and take out your spelling book for a spelling lesson." Any interest the student had in reading the library book is immediately lost.

There are reports of secondary students and adults who have never read a novel. Because many homes do not provide a model of extensive reading, the school must fill that void. Even if students have an at-home reading model, they can increase their knowledge along with their reading skills through additional in-school, sanctioned silent reading for enjoyment.

Thirty minutes per school day is a reasonable amount of time to foster the concept of recreational reading. This time span also gives you an opportunity to work on a one-to-one basis with students to incorporate remedial reading assistance for those having difficulty, enrichment for gifted readers, and help for all students between the two extremes. The Recreational Reading Module provides a base structure for teacher and students to follow; however, the structure is sufficiently flexible to accommodate the reading interests and abilities of any student in the class.

ROTATION OF BOOKS BETWEEN CLASSROOM AND LIBRARY

The Recreational Reading Module endorses bringing large numbers of library books into the classroom and

SELECTED TITLES OF BOOKS READ BY A CLASS DURING ONE RECREATIONAL READING MODULE

Herbie Goes to Monte Carlo

It's Not the End of the World

Are You There God? It's Me, Margaret

Meet John F. Kennedy

Summer Pony

Encyclopedia Brown Solves Them All

Dorrie and the Blue Witch

Dorrie and the Haunted House

Tales of a 4th Grade Nothing

A Closer Look at Prehistoric Animals

Cats: Little Tiger in Your House

Encyclopedia Brown Finds the Clue

Betsy and Mr. Kilpatrick

Rocks and Minerals

We Were There at the Battle of Britain

Understanding Money

Mysteries for Crime Busters

Benjie and His Friends

Namu

Mrs. Piggle Wiggle

Dorrie and the Goblin

Pilot Jack Knight

Sabre Jet Ace

Cases of Sherlock Holmes

Lassie Come Home

Great American Fighter Pilots of World War II

On the Edge

Hunting Grizzly Bears

The Dragons of Blueland

Shep

SELECTED TITLES OF BOOKS READ BY A DIFFERENT CLASS DURING ONE RECREATIONAL READING MODULE

Unknown Soldier

The Rocking Chair Ghost

Fun With Magic

The Jazz Man

A Doll for Lily Belle

Pinocchio

Betsy's Winter House

My Father's Dragon

Captain Smudge

I Love You, Mary Jane

Betty Crocker Cook Book

Charlotte's Web

Me and Fat Glenda

School Room Zoo

B is for Betsy

My Aunt Rosie

Mrs. Piggle Wiggle

The Shore Road Mystery

The Clue in the Embers

Funny Bones

The Mushroom Center Disaster

The Bermuda Triangle

It Could Be Worse

Here Comes the Bus

Henry and the Clubhouse

Four Donkeys

Runaway Dog, Runaway Horse

King Arthur and His Knights

Strawberry Girl

Merry Christmas

Stop! Stop!

Rabbit Cups, Monkey Tails

Say It Fast

Here Comes Pop

Do You See Mouse?

The Pet Show

The Littlest Witch

Over the Brick Wall

The Squirrel Wife

The Rodeo

Footprints Under the Window

The Defenders

Book of Riddles

Lobster King

Ball Point Banana

Henry Huggins

The Bears' Christmas

Ramona the Pest

Sharks

exchanging them frequently for other books. The teacher and librarian must have a close working relationship in at least three areas of the *Success* program: (1) establishing and developing the classroom mini-library; (2) individualizing student selection of books during regularly scheduled classes in the library; (3) assisting students in locating printed materials concerning the specific topics in the Study Skills Module.

The classroom mini-library should consist of a minimum of 50 library books, including both fiction and nonfiction. These books should be placed in each upper elementary classroom for use in the Recreational Reading Module. At least every *three* weeks, exchange the books for 50 new titles. Continue this frequent exchange throughout the school year.

In addition to the 50 books placed in the classroom, each student should go to the library on a regular basis to select and check out books.

The types of titles selected by class members is interesting to note. Above are two lists of titles of library books being read in two fourth-grade classes on the same day during the Recreational Reading Module.

Some students who select short books can read more than one during a 30-minute Recreational Reading period. Students who become engrossed in a Dr. Doolittle, Nancy Drew, *Charlotte's Web*, or *Bermuda Triangle*-length book do not want to start another book until they have finished the one they are reading, and they may select a number of shorter books later on.

The kinds of books selected by students change during the year.

In the books just listed, some students were reading the same titles. The most influential technique for getting students to read a certain title is for a class member to tell another student that he or she liked a book very much.

Another approach to capturing students' interest in reading a specific book is for you to comment favorably on the book. Overall, however, students seem to search for titles depending on either a current interest (which may fade shortly) or because they are attracted to a particular book as they browse through many library books.

THE SUSTAINED SILENT READING CONSTRUCT

With the exception of conferences between the teacher and individual students, the Recreational Reading Module is a time during the day for quiet reading. Its purpose is to maximize conditions for students to get "lost" in books. Stress the "quiet for reading" concept beginning with the first lesson.

This is *not* the time of day for oral reading by students to other students, for oral reading by the teacher to the class, or for student writing. It is *not* the time for students to ask for pronunciation and/or definitions of words. Those kinds of questions can be asked after the module. It is also *not* the time for the teacher to complete paper work at his or her desk. Students are to read books, *not* comics, newspapers, or magazines.

When a student begins a book and decides he or she does not like it, that student should go quietly, without interrupting others, to the places in the classroom where the books are kept, exchange the book for another, return to his or her desk, and begin reading.

THE TEACHER MODEL

At the beginning of the program, you should read a novel brought from home for at least five consecutive days, to establish a model of an adult reading for pleasure. Many students have never seen an adult read a novel for enjoyment. Unfortunately, many students also have never seen a teacher read for pleasure, and may think teachers only read educational materials.

THE STUDENT-TEACHER CONFERENCE

You may begin student-teacher conferences as soon as you have established the model of quiet reading of individually selected fiction and nonfiction. The class should realize that this 30-minute segment is a time not to interrupt anyone else, nor to be interrupted.

Hold a conference between you and one student for approximately ten minutes. Conferences with three different students can be held during this module each day.

A conference focus guide is provided for this module in each lesson in Appendix One. The focus is repeated for several days to afford time for you to have a conference with each student in the class regarding that focus, before moving to a different focus. You should adjust the number of days needed for a particular conference focus, depending on the number of students in the class.

Each conference has two major purposes: (1) to provide time for an adult to talk with a student individually about reading interests and dislikes, and (2) to provide time for that adult to check word analysis and reading comprehension skills with an individual student *using the student's fiction or nonfiction library books*.

Here are suggested questions to use in the conference to supplement the specific conference focus noted in the Recreational Reading Modules:

1. What do you like to read about?
2. What is the best book you've read since our last conference?
3. Why was it a good book?
4. What is the saddest book you've ever read?
5. Why was it sad?
6. What is the most exciting book you've ever read?
7. What parts were exciting?
8. What kind of characters do you like best?
9. What kind of book have you never read?
10. What books would you recommend to a friend to read? Why?

Figure 5–1 is a suggested form for you to use to jot down notes concerning a student during the conference.

THE CYCLES

In the Recreational Reading Module, the cycles

DATE	EMPHASIS AND COMMENTS *	MASTERY OF SKILL	NEEDS MORE PRACTICE
STUDENT'S NAME *Rodney Stedmont*			
9/1	Parts of Books (favorite books are mysteries and chase stories)	Yes	
9/18	Locate subjects and predicates		Especially predicates

FIGURE 5–1 Recreational Reading Conference Notes

*Teacher selects a word analysis and/or comprehension skill or uses the one identified in the Recreational Reading Module in the lesson in Appendix One.

emphasize a word analysis or reading comprehension skill. This becomes a part of the student-teacher conference. Tables 5–1 and 5–2 list cycle emphases and the lesson numbers for the first and second halves of the academic year. These are a minimum of emphases. You will need to add additional topics during the teacher-student conference. These cycles afford a base which each teacher can expand, and the lists should be helpful in planning.

SEQUENCE FOR TEACHING THE MODULE

Here is a suggested format to use during this module each day.

1. Each student selects a fiction or nonfiction library book and records the date, title of the book, and the number of the first page to be read that day on a form such as the one in Figure 5–2.
2. During the first days of the program, read an adult novel silently while all students read their books.

TABLE 5–1 Recreational Reading Cycles, First Half of Academic Year, Lessons 1–90

Cycle	Lessons	Emphasis
1	1–4	Teacher model
2	5–10	Parts and features of library books
3	11–20	Subjects and predicates
4	21–30	Recognizing different kinds of paragraphs
5	31–40	Pronouns
6	41–50	Dialogue
7	51–60	Nouns
8	61–70	Characters
9	71–80	Apostrophes
10	81–90	Pronouns

TABLE 5–2 Recreational Reading Cycles, Second Half of Academic Year, Lessons 91–180

Cycle	Lessons	Emphasis
11	91–100	Causes, effects, comprehension of plots
12	101–112	Parts of speech
13	113–120	Character analysis, realism, fantasy
14	121–130	Locating social studies information, prefixes, suffixes
15	131–140	Identifying sentence structure
16	141–150	Locating science information
17	151–160	Word definition in context
18	161–170	Drawing conclusions
19	171–180	Locating mathematics and/or health information

FIGURE 5–2   Fiction and Nonfiction Books Read

Student's Name

Date	Title of Book	Started on Page	Ended on Page

3. Thereafter, have three student/teacher conferences during this module. Ask one student to come to the desk and bring books he or she has read or is now reading. The conference lasts for approximately ten minutes, and the student does no writing during the conference. Repeat the procedure with two other students.

   Refer to the Recreational Reading Module in the lessons in Appendix One for one specific emphasis area to use in the conference. This area should be repeated for several days so each student will have an opportunity to discuss it with you. The only talking in the room should be from the conference.

4. At the end of the 30 minutes, the student completes the record sheet by writing the number of the last page read. In some classrooms, the record was filed in a box; other teachers asked students to keep the most current sheet at their desks, and pages that had been completed were filed in a folder kept in a box labeled *Recreational Reading*.

References

Duff, Annis. *Bequest of Wings*. New York: Viking Press, 1944.

Huck, Charlotte. *Children's Literature in the Elementary School*. New York: Holt, Rinehart and Winston, 1976.

Moore, Anne Carroll. *My Roads to Childhood*. Boston: Horn Book Co., 1961.

Perrine, Laurence. *Story and Structure*. New York: Harcourt Brace Jovanovich, 1974.

Smith, Irene. *A History of the Newbery and Caldecott Medals*. New York: Viking Press, 1957.

Whitehead, Robert. *Children's Literature: Strategies of Teaching*. Englewood Cliffs, N.J.: Prentice-Hall, 1968.

appendix one
The Lessons

PHASE 1—INTRODUCTORY PHASE—LESSONS 1–10

LESSON 1

Phonics/Spelling

CYCLE 1: PART 1: INTRODUCTORY DISCUSSIONS

VOCABULARY EMPHASIS: Words or phrases related to school opening, including names of teacher, principal, school, etc.

HOMEWORK: Team test your spelling words with a parent. Parent signs notebook.

Composition

CYCLE 1: WRITING COMPLETE SENTENCES

PREWRITING: Write "People do different things." on the chalkboard and mark the subject/predicate in that sentence. Have students suggest sentences about different things that people do. Write these sentences on the chalkboard. Mark subject/predicate in each sentence.

WRITING ASSIGNMENT: Students write sentences related to the theme of the lesson.

PROOFREADING THRUST: Check at least one *subject and predicate* in a sentence.

Study Skills

CYCLE 1: ALPHABETIZING THEME: People

MATERIAL: Student handbook or printed list of school personnel or roll sheet

READING ASSIGNMENT: Read to find names of people.

WRITING ASSIGNMENT: Alphabetize the names of some classmates or school personnel.

Recreational Reading

CYCLE 1: TEACHER ESTABLISHING MODEL

Everyone, including the teacher, reads fiction or nonfiction books silently.

LESSON 2

Phonics/Spelling

VOCABULARY EMPHASIS: Words or phrases related to expectations about the new school year.

HOMEWORK: Team test your spelling words with a parent. Parent signs notebook.

Composition

PREWRITING: Discuss daily and weekly schedules. Write examples in sentences on the chalkboard. Mark subject/predicate in each sentence.

WRITING ASSIGNMENT: Write sentences about daily and weekly schedules.

PROOFREADING THRUST: Check the *subject/predicate* in a sentence.

Study Skills

THEME: People

MATERIAL: Social studies textbook

READING ASSIGNMENT: Read to locate names of famous people.

WRITING ASSIGNMENT: Make a list of names and put the names in alphabetical order, or write some facts about one famous person.

Recreational Reading

TEACHER ESTABLISHING MODEL: Everyone, including the teacher, reads fiction or nonfiction books silently.

LESSON 3

Phonics/Spelling

VOCABULARY EMPHASIS: Words or phrases related to *cafeteria*.

HOMEWORK: Team test your spelling words with a parent. Parent signs notebook.

Composition

PREWRITING: Write "A monster came to school today." on the chalkboard as an example of a simple subject in a sentence. Mark the subject.

WRITING ASSIGNMENT: Write sentences about the monster.

PROOFREADING THRUST: Check the *subject* in a sentence.

HOMEWORK: Assign appropriate pages in a language textbook or worksheet about simple subjects.

Study Skills

THEME: People

MATERIAL: Newspapers

READING ASSIGNMENT: Read the headlines in the newspaper with people's names.

WRITING ASSIGNMENT: Copy three headlines. Put the words from the headlines in alphabetical order.

Recreational Reading

TEACHER ESTABLISHING MODEL: Everyone, including the teacher, reads fiction or nonfiction books silently.

LESSON 4

Phonics/Spelling

VOCABULARY EMPHASIS: Words or phrases related to school bus safety or traffic safety.

HOMEWORK: Team test your spelling words with a parent. Parent signs notebook.

Composition

PREWRITING: Write "Football season started today." on the chalkboard and mark the verb. Students volunteer sentences about football season. Mark the verb in each sentence.

WRITING ASSIGNMENT: Write sentences about the theme sentence.

PROOFREADING THRUST: Check at least one *verb*.

HOMEWORK: Teacher copies on a stencil several sentences written by students. Students mark verbs in each sentence.

Study Skills

THEME: People

MATERIAL: Newspapers

READING ASSIGNMENT: Read to find words about people. The words should begin with the same letter.

WRITING ASSIGNMENT: Make a list of the words and put them in alphabetical order.

Recreational Reading

TEACHER ESTABLISHING MODEL: Everyone, including the teacher, reads fiction or nonfiction books silently.

LESSON 5

Phonics/Spelling

VOCABULARY EMPHASIS: Words or phrases related to use of library, including reference and resource materials.

HOMEWORK: Team test your spelling words with a parent. Parent signs notebook.

Composition

PREWRITING: Write "Many people are important to me." on the chalkboard. Write sentences volunteered by students about the theme sentence, emphasize any "being" verbs.

WRITING ASSIGNMENT: Students write additional sentences about the theme. Some sentences should contain a "being" verb.

PROOFREADING THRUST: Check at least one *"being"* verb.

HOMEWORK: Assign appropriate pages in textbook about "being" verbs.

Study Skills

THEME: Food Products

MATERIAL: Magazines

READING ASSIGNMENT: Read to locate food products.

WRITING ASSIGNMENT: Make a list of the products and then put them in alphabetical order.

HOMEWORK: Find products at home that begin with the same letter.

Recreational Reading

CYCLE 2: PARTS AND FEATURES OF LIBRARY BOOKS Begin conferences with three individual students. Each conference should last approximately 10 minutes. During the conference, include a discussion of *parts and features* of the library books brought to the conference by each student.

LESSON 6

Phonics/Spelling

VOCABULARY EMPHASIS: Words or phrases that describe the classroom.

HOMEWORK: Team test your spelling words with a parent. Parent signs notebook.

Composition

PREWRITING: Write "I have a pet dinosaur." on the chalkboard. Mark the subject/predicate in the sentence. Students suggest other sentences.

WRITING ASSIGNMENT: Students write sentences about dinosaurs or make-believe pets.

PROOFREADING THRUST: Check *capital letters* at beginning of sentence and *punctuation* at end.

Study Skills

THEME: Food Products

MATERIAL: Encyclopedias

READING ASSIGNMENT: Select any food to read about in your volume of an encyclopedia.

WRITING ASSIGNMENT: Write the *guide words* at the top of the page you were reading. Write at least two facts you learned about the food product.

Recreational Reading

PARTS AND FEATURES OF LIBRARY BOOKS: During the 10 minute conference with three individual students, include a discussion of *parts and features* of the library books brought to the conference by each student.

LESSON 7

Phonics/Spelling

VOCABULARY EMPHASIS: Words or phrases related to subjects studied.

HOMEWORK: Team test your spelling words with a parent. Parent signs notebook.

Composition

PREWRITING: Discuss "self." Write sentences volunteered by students about themselves.

WRITING ASSIGNMENT: Describe yourself. Do not give your name. Write your name on the back of the paper.

PROOFREADING THRUST: Check capitalization of the pronoun *I*.

Study Skills

THEME: Food products

MATERIAL: Dictionary

READING ASSIGNMENT: Skim the dictionary to find foods that begin with *t*.

WRITING ASSIGNMENT: Write the foods in a list. Write the *guide words* from the pages on which the words were found.

Recreational Reading

PARTS AND FEATURES OF LIBRARY BOOKS: During the 10 minute conference with three individual students, include a discussion of *parts and features* of the library books brought to the conference by each student.

HOMEWORK: Read at home for at least 15 minutes in any material you choose. Ask a parent to sign a note, "——————— read for ——— minutes tonight."

LESSON 8

Phonics/Spelling

VOCABULARY EMPHASIS: Words or phrases related to classroom schedules and the days of the week.

HOMEWORK: Team test your spelling words with a parent. Parent signs notebook.

Composition

PREWRITING: Discuss things liked and disliked.

WRITING ASSIGNMENT: Write sentences telling why you like or dislike certain things.

PROOFREADING THRUST: Check *verbs* in sentences.

Study Skills

THEME: Addition and subtraction

MATERIAL: Mathematics textbooks

READING ASSIGNMENT: Read to locate words associated with addition and subtraction.

WRITING ASSIGNMENT: Make a list of the words. Put the words in alphabetical order.

Recreational Reading

PARTS AND FEATURES OF LIBRARY BOOKS: During the 10 minute conference with three individual students, include a discussion of *parts and features* of the library books brought to the conference by each student.

LESSON 9

Phonics/Spelling

VOCABULARY EMPHASIS: Words or phrases related to events of the first half of the school year and/or first six months of the year.

HOMEWORK: Team test your spelling words with a parent. Parent signs notebook.

Composition

PREWRITING: Discuss dreams.

WRITING ASSIGNMENT: Write sentences about dreams.

PROOFREADING THRUST: Underline *pronouns* in sentences.

Study Skills

THEME: Characters, towns, and cities

MATERIAL: Fiction books

READING ASSIGNMENT: Read to locate names of characters in the book and a place associated with each.

WRITING ASSIGNMENT: Put in alphabetical order all the places found.

Recreational Reading

PARTS AND FEATURES OF LIBRARY BOOKS: During the 10 minute conference with three individual students, include a discussion of *parts and features* of the library books brought to the conference by each student.

LESSON 10

Phonics/Spelling

VOCABULARY EMPHASIS: Words or phrases related to important aspects of the school year and/or last six months of the year. Or Chart Review Test

HOMEWORK: Team test your spelling words with a parent. Parent signs notebook.

Composition

PREWRITING: Discuss exteriors of buildings. Or Sharing Day

WRITING ASSIGNMENT: Write advantages and disadvantages of at least one kind of building exterior.

PROOFREADING THRUST: Use at least one word to denote *time* in the writing.

Study Skills

THEME: Towns and cities

MATERIAL: Television guide

READING ASSIGNMENT: Read to locate names of programs that have a town or city in the title.

WRITING ASSIGNMENT: Alphabetize the titles you listed using the first word in the title. If the first words are the same, go to the second word, etc.

Recreational Reading

PARTS AND FEATURES OF LIBRARY BOOKS: During the 10 minute conference with three individual students, include a discussion of *parts and features* of the library books brought to the conference by each student.

PHASE 2—TRANSITION PHASE—LESSONS 11–40

LESSON 11

Phonics/Spelling

CYCLE 1, PART 2:
CURRENT
EVENTS VOCAB-
ULARY WITH
SPELLING
EMPHASIS

SPELLING EMPHA-
SIS: *gr*

VOCABULARY
EMPHASIS:
People

MATERIAL: *Time*
and *Newsweek*,
other magazines

HOMEWORK: Team
test your spelling
words with a par-
ent. Parent signs
notebook.

Composition

CYCLE 2: USING CORRECT
VERB FORMS IN SEN-
TENCES

PREWRITING: Discuss big
things. Take sentences about
big things. Point out verbs.

WRITING ASSIGNMENT: Write
sentences about big things.

PROOFREADING THRUST: Use
a *verb* in every sentence.

HOMEWORK: Language text-
book—locate and complete sub-
ject/verb assignment.

Study Skills

THEME: National
parks and recreation
facilities

MATERIAL: Maps

READING ASSIGN-
MENT: Read to
locate names of
national parks and
recreation facilities.
Students may work
in pairs; however,
each student writes
his or her own
paper.

WRITING ASSIGN-
MENT: Write the
names of parks and
recreation facilities
in alphabetical
order.

Recreational Reading

CYCLE 3: SUB-
JECTS AND
PREDICATES
During the 10 min-
ute conference with
three individual
students, include a
discussion of *sub-
jects and predicates*
found by the stu-
dent in his or her
library books.

LESSON 12

Phonics/Spelling

SPELLING EMPHA-
SIS: Consonant
cluster *pr*

VOCABULARY
EMPHASIS:
People

MATERIAL: *Time*
and *Newsweek*,
other magazines

HOMEWORK: Team
test your spelling
words with a par-
ent. Parent signs
notebook.

Composition

PREWRITING: Discuss a big fat
turkey. Point out the verbs of
"being" on board.

WRITING ASSIGNMENT: Write
a creative story about a turkey.

PROOFREADING THRUST:
Begin at least one sentence with
"If . . ."

HOMEWORK: Verb of "being"
activity.

Study Skills

CYCLE 2:
SEQUENCE

THEME: Recipes

MATERIAL: Labels
from food, recipe
cards, magazine
recipes

READING ASSIGN-
MENT: Read direc-
tions for preparing
one food.

WRITING ASSIGN-
MENT: Write the
steps that should be
taken to prepare the
food and number
each step. The stu-
dent should use his
or her own words.

Recreational Reading

SUBJECTS AND
PREDICATES:
During the 10 min-
ute conference with
three individual
students, include a
discussion of *sub-
jects and predicates*
found by the stu-
dent in his or her
library books.

LESSON 13

Phonics/Spelling

SPELLING EMPHASIS: Consonant cluster *gl*

VOCABULARY EMPHASIS: Sports

MATERIAL: Newspapers

HOMEWORK: Team test your spelling words with a parent. Parent signs notebook.

Composition

PREWRITING: Discuss a favorite relative. Emphasize singular, subject/"being" verb relationship in example sentences.

WRITING ASSIGNMENT: Write sentences about a favorite relative.

PROOFREADING THRUST: At least one sentence should have a singular *subject*.

HOMEWORK: Write sentences about your family using *is, am, are, was, were*. Make sure you use singular and plural subjects.

Study Skills

THEME: Television

MATERIAL: Television viewing or TV guide

READING ASSIGNMENT: Students recall from memory or read in TV guide programs watched.

WRITING ASSIGNMENT: Make a schedule for your television viewing for one night. List the times and programs watched.

Recreational Reading

SUBJECTS AND PREDICATES: During the 10 minute conference with three individual students, include a discussion of *subjects and predicates* found by the student in his or her library books.

LESSON 14

Phonics/Spelling

SPELLING EMPHA-SIS: Consonant cluster *fl*

VOCABULARY EMPHASIS: Nature

MATERIAL: News-papers

HOMEWORK: Team test your spelling words with a parent. Parent signs notebook.

Composition

PREWRITING: Discuss special friends. Discuss plural subject/verb relationship in example sentences.

WRITING ASSIGNMENT: Write a paragraph about special friends.

PROOFREADING THRUST: Use *because* in at least one sentence.

Study Skills

THEME: Science project

MATERIAL: Science textbooks

READING ASSIGN-MENT: Read to locate a science project you could do at home.

WRITING ASSIGN-MENT: Write the steps in order needed to do the project.

Recreational Reading

SUBJECTS AND PREDICATES: During the 10 minute conference with three individual students, include a discussion of *subjects and predicates* found by the student in his or her library books.

LESSON 15

Phonics/Spelling

SPELLING EMPHA-SIS: Consonant cluster *sm*

VOCABULARY EMPHASIS: Money

MATERIAL: News-papers

HOMEWORK: Team test your spelling words with a parent. Parent signs notebook.

Composition

PREWRITING: Discuss "The Magic Racecar." Emphasize the use of past tense verbs.

WRITING ASSIGNMENT: Begin a story about a magic racecar using past tense verbs. (two-day time-lapse writing)

PROOFREADING THRUST: Use at least one past tense *verb* in a sentence.

Study Skills

THEME: Historical events

MATERIAL: Social studies textbooks

READING ASSIGN-MENT: Read to locate interesting facts about historical events.

WRITING ASSIGN-MENT: Make a list of these events in proper sequence.

Recreational Reading

SUBJECTS AND PREDICATES: During the 10 minute conference with three individual students, include a discussion of *subjects and predicates* found by the student in his or her library books.

100

LESSON 16

Phonics/Spelling

SPELLING EMPHA-
SIS: Consonant
cluster *sc*

VOCABULARY
EMPHASIS:
Weather

MATERIAL: News-
papers

HOMEWORK: Stu-
dents use words
they choose to spell
in sentences.

Composition

PREWRITING: Continue discussion of "The Magic Racecar."
Discuss action verbs.

WRITING ASSIGNMENT: Com-
plete story started yesterday.

PROOFREADING THRUST: Use
at least one *s-form of a verb* in a
sentence.

HOMEWORK: Language text-
book activity related to subject/
verb agreement.

Study Skills

THEME: Activities at
home

MATERIAL: Newspa-
pers, scissors, con-
struction paper, glue
or paste

READING ASSIGN-
MENT: Read to
locate a cartoon with
captions that indi-
cates something hap-
pening at home.

WRITING ASSIGN-
MENT: Write a
description of what
happens in each
frame of the cartoon
in correct sequence.
Cut out cartoon and
glue each frame on
paper. File to use
tomorrow.

Recreational Reading

SUBJECTS AND
PREDICATES:
During the 10 min-
ute conference with
three individual
students, include a
discussion of *sub-
jects and predicates*
found by the stu-
dent in his or her
library books.

LESSON 17

Phonics/Spelling

SPELLING EMPHASIS: Consonant cluster *fr*

VOCABULARY EMPHASIS: Weather

MATERIAL: *Time* and *Newsweek*, other magazines

HOMEWORK: Students use words they choose to spell in sentences.

Composition

PREWRITING: Discuss "The Runaway School Bus." Emphasize the use of helping verbs.

WRITING ASSIGNMENT: Write sentences or paragraphs about "The Runaway School Bus."

PROOFREADING THRUST: Underline *plural* words.

Study Skills

THEME: Activities at home

MATERIAL: Newspaper work continued from previous lesson

READING ASSIGNMENT: Students work in pairs, trade cartoons prepared yesterday, and read frames.

WRITING ASSIGNMENT: Write in sentences what is happening in the frames.

Recreational Reading

SUBJECTS AND PREDICATES: During the 10 minute conference with three individual students, include a discussion of *subjects and predicates* found by the student in his or her library books.

LESSON 18

Phonics/Spelling

SPELLING EMPHA-SIS: Consonant cluster *sk*

VOCABULARY EMPHASIS: Sports

MATERIAL: *Time* and *Newsweek,* other magazines

HOMEWORK: Students use words they choose to spell in sentences.

Composition

PREWRITING: Discuss "Kim, the Computer." Illustrate expansion of simple sentence using student examples.

WRITING ASSIGNMENT: Write a creative paragraph or story about a computer named Kim.

PROOFREADING THRUST: At least one sentence should begin with *when.*

HOMEWORK: Take home a newspaper page. Circle different verb tenses.

Study Skills

CYCLE 3: FINDING BASIC FACTS

THEME: Events and people

MATERIAL: Magazines

READING ASSIGN-MENT: Read an article about a person and/or event to find *who, what, when, where* in the article.

WRITING ASSIGN-MENT: Answer *who, what, when, where* about the article in your own words in complete sentences.

Recreational Reading

SUBJECTS AND PREDICATES: During the 10 minute conference with three individual students, include a discussion of *subjects and predicates* found by the student in his or her library books.

LESSON 19

Phonics/Spelling

SPELLING EMPHA-
SIS: Consonant
cluster *sp*

VOCABULARY
EMPHASIS:
Entertainment

MATERIAL: News-
papers

HOMEWORK: Stu-
dents use words
they choose to spell
in sentences.

Composition

PREWRITING: Discuss "Strange
Tracks."

WRITING ASSIGNMENT: Write
sentences about strange tracks
by your window.

PROOFREADING THRUST: Use
did and/or *done* correctly in a
sentence.

Study Skills

THEME: Events and
people

MATERIAL: Encyclo-
pedias

READING ASSIGN-
MENT: Select a per-
son or event to read
to locate basic facts:
*who, what, when,
where.*

WRITING ASSIGN-
MENT: Answer
*who, what, when,
where* questions
about your subject.

Recreational Reading

SUBJECTS AND
PREDICATES:
During the 10 min-
ute conference with
three individual
students, include a
discussion of *sub-
jects and predicates*
found by the stu-
dent in his or her
library books.

LESSON 20

Phonics/Spelling

SPELLING EMPHA-
SIS: Consonant
cluster *st*

VOCABULARY
EMPHASIS: Food.
Or Chart Review
Test

MATERIAL: News-
papers

HOMEWORK: Stu-
dents use words
they choose to spell
in sentences.

Composition

PREWRITING: Discuss Shark! Or
Sharing Day

WRITING ASSIGNMENT: Write
a creative story about a shark.

PROOFREADING THRUST: Use
have, had, or *has* as a *helping
verb* in at least one sentence.

Study Skills

THEME: Events and
people

MATERIAL: Diction-
ary

READING ASSIGN-
MENT: Read to
locate names of peo-
ple and to find basic
facts about them.

WRITING ASSIGN-
MENT: Write
answers to *who,
what, when, where*
questions about the
persons and facts you
located.

Recreational Reading

SUBJECTS AND
PREDICATES:
During the 10 min-
ute conference with
three individual
students, include a
discussion of *sub-
jects and predicates*
found by the stu-
dent in his or her
library books.

LESSON 21

Phonics/Spelling

SPELLING EMPHA-SIS: Consonant cluster *dr*

VOCABULARY EMPHASIS: Transportation

MATERIAL: Newspapers

HOMEWORK: Students use words they choose to spell in sentences.

Composition

CYCLE 3: WRITING DESCRIPTIONS

PREWRITING: Discuss positive ways to describe people—physical appearance, actions, etc.

WRITING ASSIGNMENT: Write sentences describing a classmate.

PROOFREADING THRUST: Use at least one *adjective*.

Study Skills

THEME: Events and people

MATERIAL: Mathematics textbooks

READING ASSIGNMENT: Read title page of mathematics textbook.

WRITING ASSIGNMENT: Answer *who, what, when, where* questions concerning publication of text with information from title page.

Recreational Reading

CYCLE 4: RECOGNIZING DIFFERENT KINDS OF PARAGRAPHS Include in the conference a discussion of *different kinds of paragraphs*—short, long, paragraphs with dialogue, paragraphs containing descriptions, etc.

LESSON 22

Phonics/Spelling

SPELLING EMPHA-SIS: Consonant cluster *sw*

VOCABULARY EMPHASIS: Vacations

MATERIAL: Newspapers

HOMEWORK: Students use words they choose to spell in sentences.

Composition

PREWRITING: Discuss an automobile trip. Emphasize use of senses.

WRITING ASSIGNMENT: Write a paragraph to describe an airplane trip.

PROOFREADING THRUST: Use at least one word to denote *sensory perceptions*.

Study Skills

THEME: Characters in books

MATERIAL: Fiction books, comic books

READING ASSIGNMENT: Read to find facts about a main character.

WRITING ASSIGNMENT: Answer *who, what, when, where* questions about the character.

Recreational Reading

RECOGNIZING DIFFERENT KINDS OF PARAGRAPHS: Include in the conference a discussion of *different kinds of paragraphs*—short, long, paragraphs with dialogue, paragraphs containing descriptions, etc.

LESSON 23

Phonics/Spelling

SPELLING EMPHASIS: Consonant cluster *ance*

VOCABULARY EMPHASIS: Health

MATERIAL: *Time* and *Newsweek*, other magazines

HOMEWORK: Students use words they choose to spell in sentences.

Composition

PREWRITING: Discuss food. (May bring certain foods to taste.)

WRITING ASSIGNMENT: Describe a food you like, in detail.

PROOFREADING THRUST: Use *commas* to separate words in a series.

Study Skills

THEME: Advertisements

MATERIAL: Telephone book yellow pages

READING ASSIGNMENT: Read advertisements to find basic facts about a service or product people need.

WRITING ASSIGNMENT: Answer *who, what, when, where* questions about at least one advertisement.

Recreational Reading

RECOGNIZING DIFFERENT KINDS OF PARAGRAPHS: Include in the conference a discussion of *different kinds of paragraphs*—short, long, paragraphs with dialogue, paragraphs containing descriptions, etc.

LESSON 24

Phonics/Spelling

SPELLING EMPHASIS: Consonant cluster *bl*

VOCABULARY EMPHASIS: World affairs

MATERIAL: *Time* and *Newsweek*, other magazines

HOMEWORK: Students use words they choose to spell in sentences.

Composition

PREWRITING: Describe any *object* without naming the object.

WRITING ASSIGNMENT: Write an "I Spy" description of an object in the classroom that all can see.

PROOFREADING THRUST: Give accurate *details* in the description.

Study Skills

CYCLE 4: MAKING CHARTS AND TABLES

THEME: Traveling

MATERIAL: Maps

READING ASSIGNMENT: Read mileage chart on a map.

WRITING ASSIGNMENT: Make a chart to show mileage for some trips you would like to take. Example:

FROM	TO	MILES

Recreational Reading

RECOGNIZING DIFFERENT KINDS OF PARAGRAPHS: Include in the conference a discussion of *different kinds of paragraphs*—short, long, paragraphs with dialogue, paragraphs containing descriptions, etc.

LESSON 25

Phonics/Spelling

SPELLING EMPHA-
SIS: Consonant
cluster *fr*
VOCABULARY
EMPHASIS: Travel
MATERIAL: News-
papers
HOMEWORK: Stu-
dents use words
they choose to spell
in sentences.

Composition

PREWRITING: Describe favorite
television stars.
WRITING ASSIGNMENT: Write
a description of your favorite
television personality.
PROOFREADING THRUST: A
proper *noun* in a sentence.

Study Skills

THEME: Traveling
MATERIAL: Travel
folders or travel
advertisements in
magazines
READING ASSIGN-
MENT: Read travel
information to plan a
trip. Locate as many
items of expense as
possible.
WRITING ASSIGN-
MENT: Make a
chart to show travel
plans and possible
costs. Example:

PLAN	COST
Airfare	$190,000
Hotel	40,000
etc.	

Recreational Reading

RECOGNIZING
DIFFERENT
KINDS OF PARA-
GRAPHS: Include
in the conference a
discussion of *differ-
ent kinds of para-
graphs*—short,
long, paragraphs
with dialogue, para-
graphs containing
descriptions, etc.

LESSON 26

Phonics/Spelling

SPELLING EMPHA-SIS: Consonant cluster *str*

VOCABULARY EMPHASIS: Travel

MATERIAL: Newspapers

HOMEWORK: Students use words they choose to spell in sentences.

Composition

CYCLE 4: WRITING COMPARI-SONS

PREWRITING: Discuss how things are alike and different.

WRITING ASSIGNMENT: Each student writes about how two objects on their desk are alike and different.

PROOFREADING THRUST: Check a *noun*.

HOMEWORK: Select foods you ate at home today and write about their similarities and differences.

Study Skills

THEME: Transportation

MATERIAL: Newspaper

READING ASSIGN-MENT: Read in the newspaper for words relating to transportation

WRITING ASSIGN-MENT: Make a list of transportation words. Make a chart to put these words into categories.

Recreational Reading

RECOGNIZING DIFFERENT KINDS OF PARA-GRAPHS: Include in the conference a discussion of *different kinds of paragraphs*—short, long, paragraphs with dialogue, paragraphs containing descriptions, etc.

LESSON 27

Phonics/Spelling

SPELLING EMPHA-SIS: Consonant clusters *dw, tw*

VOCABULARY EMPHASIS: Public announcements

MATERIAL: Newspapers

HOMEWORK: Students use words they choose to spell in sentences.

Composition

PREWRITING: Discuss different kinds of animals.

WRITING ASSIGNMENT: Write a comparison of at least two animals.

PROOFREADING THRUST: Check a common *noun*.

Study Skills

THEME: Transportation

MATERIAL: Science and health textbooks

READING ASSIGN-MENT: Read to locate words associated with travel.

WRITING ASSIGN-MENT: Make a chart to list information found. Example:

BOOK	PAGES	TRAVEL WORDS

Recreational Reading

RECOGNIZING DIFFERENT KINDS OF PARA-GRAPHS: Include in the conference a discussion of *different kinds of paragraphs*—short, long, paragraphs with dialogue, paragraphs containing descriptions, etc.

LESSON 28

Phonics/Spelling

SPELLING EMPHA-
SIS: Consonant
cluster *st* in at least
one word in each
sentence
VOCABULARY
EMPHASIS: Travel
MATERIAL: News-
papers
HOMEWORK: Stu-
dents use words
they choose to spell
in sentences.

Composition

PREWRITING: Discuss seasons.
WRITING ASSIGNMENT:
Write a comparison of any
two seasons.
PROOFREADING THRUST: Use
at least two *color words*.

Study Skills

THEME: Trans-
portation
MATERIAL: Social
studies textbooks
READING ASSIGN-
MENT: Read to
locate different
means of transporta-
tion in history.
WRITING ASSIGN-
MENT: Make a
chart to show the
mode of travel,
date(s) in history,
people using this
mode of travel.
Example:

MODE	DATE(S)	WHO USES

Recreational Reading

RECOGNIZING
DIFFERENT
KINDS OF PARA-
GRAPHS: Include
in the conference a
discussion of *differ-
ent kinds of para-
graphs*—short,
long, paragraphs
with dialogue, para-
graphs containing
descriptions, etc.

LESSON 29

Phonics/Spelling

SPELLING EMPHA-
SIS: Consonant
cluster *cl* in at least
one word in each
sentence

VOCABULARY
EMPHASIS: Rec-
reation

MATERIAL: *Time*
and *Newsweek*,
other magazines

HOMEWORK: Stu-
dents use words
they choose to spell
in sentences.

Composition

PREWRITING: Discuss plants
and animals.

WRITING ASSIGNMENT: Write
a comparison of plants and animals.

PROOOFREADING THRUST:
Use at least one word to denote
movement.

Study Skills

THEME: Trans-
portation

MATERIAL: News-
papers

READING ASSIGN-
MENT: Read the
used car, truck,
trailer, motorcycle,
etc. advertisements
to find costs of differ-
ent vehicles.

WRITING ASSIGN-
MENT: Make a
chart to show infor-
mation. Example:

VEHICLE	YEAR	MAKE	COST

Recreational Reading

RECOGNIZING
DIFFERENT
KINDS OF PARA-
GRAPHS: Include
in the conference a
discussion of *differ-
ent kinds of para-
graphs*—short,
long, paragraphs
with dialogue, para-
graphs containing
descriptions, etc.

LESSON 30

Phonics/Spelling

SPELLING EMPHA-
SIS: Consonant
cluster *tr* in words
in sentences

VOCABULARY
EMPHASIS: Rec-
reation

MATERIAL: *Time*
and *Newsweek*,
other magazines.
Or Chart Review
Test

HOMEWORK: Stu-
dents use words
they choose to spell
in sentences.

Composition

PREWRITING: Discuss the sun
and the moon. Or Sharing Day

WRITING ASSIGNMENT: Write
a comparison of the sun and the
moon.

PROOFREADING THRUST: A
verb in a sentence.

Study Skills

THEME: Trans-
portation

MATERIAL: News-
papers

READING ASSIGN-
MENT: Read to
locate information
about someone trav-
eling.

WRITING ASSIGN-
MENT: Make a
chart to show *who,
where, how,* and
when information
about the person
traveling. Example:

WHO	WHERE	HOW	WHEN

Recreational Reading

RECOGNIZING DIF-
FERENT KINDS
OF PARAGRAPHS:
Include in the con-
ference a discussion
of *different kinds of
paragraphs*—short,
long, paragraphs
with dialogue, para-
graphs containing
descriptions, etc.

LESSON 31

Phonics/Spelling

SPELLING EMPHASIS: Consonant cluster *wh* in 2-3 syllable words

VOCABULARY EMPHASIS: Education

MATERIAL: Newspapers

HOMEWORK: Students use words they choose to spell in sentences.

Composition

CYCLE 5: DEVELOPING PARAGRAPHS

PREWRITING: Discuss times when you have been angry.

WRITING ASSIGNMENT: Write a paragraph about a time you have been angry.

PROOFREADING THRUST: *Verbs* that add *ed* to form past tense.

Study Skills

CYCLE 5: INFORMATION FROM PICTURES

THEME: Occupations

MATERIAL: Magazines

READING ASSIGNMENT: Locate magazine pictures of people working.

WRITING ASSIGNMENT: List words or phrases that relate to the kinds of work shown in the pictures or found in the paragraphs.

Recreational Reading

CYCLE 5: PRONOUNS During each conference, ask the student to locate and discuss different *pronouns* in his or her library books.

LESSON 32

Phonics/Spelling

SPELLING EMPHASIS: *ch* in 2–3 syllable words

VOCABULARY EMPHASIS: Education

MATERIAL: Newspapers

HOMEWORK: Students use words they choose to spell in sentences.

Composition

PREWRITING: Write on the chalkboard clusters of words volunteered by the students concerning two categories— *foods* and *hobbies*.

WRITING ASSIGNMENT: Write additional phrases for each category. Develop at least one paragraph about one category.

PROOFREADING THRUST: Mark *subject and predicate* in one sentence.

Study Skills

THEME: Occupations

MATERIAL: Encyclopedias

READING ASSIGNMENT: Locate a picture of people working and read the caption and/or locate information about one kind of work.

WRITING ASSIGNMENT: Write facts learned.

Recreational Reading

PRONOUNS: During each conference, ask the student to locate and discuss different *pronouns* in his or her library book.

LESSON 33

Phonics/Spelling

SPELLING EMPHASIS: *th* in 2–3 syllable words

VOCABULARY EMPHASIS: Economics

MATERIAL: Newspapers

HOMEWORK: Students use words they choose to spell in sentences.

Composition

PREWRITING: Write "Saturday is my favorite day of the week." on the chalkboard as an example of a topic sentence. Write other possible topic sentences volunteered by students.

WRITING ASSIGNMENT: Write at least one paragraph about your favorite day.

PROOFREADING THRUST: *Indent* beginning of paragraph.

HOMEWORK: Assign textbook pages about topic sentences.

Study Skills

THEME: Occupations

MATERIAL: Dictionaries

READING ASSIGNMENT: Locate names of items people can use in their work (e.g., kinds of tools).

WRITING ASSIGNMENT: Make a list of words found and write an explanation of how each relates to a particular kind of work.

Recreational Reading

PRONOUNS: During each conference, ask the student to locate and discuss different *pronouns* in his or her library book.

LESSON 34

Phonics/Spelling

SPELLING EMPHA-SIS: *sh* in 2–3 sylla-ble words

VOCABULARY EMPHASIS: Eco-nomics

MATERIAL: News-papers

HOMEWORK: Stu-dents use words they choose to spell in sentences.

Composition

PREWRITING: Develop a para-graph on the chalkboard about rainy days.

WRITING ASSIGNMENT: Write paragraphs about rainy days.

PROOFREADING THRUST: Mark *topic sentence(s)*.

Study Skills

THEME: Money

MATERIAL: Mathe-matics textbooks

READING ASSIGN-MENT: Locate either pictures or word problems per-taining to money.

WRITING ASSIGN-MENT: Write your own word problems based on information found.

Recreational Reading

PRONOUNS: During each conference, ask the student to locate and discuss different *pronouns* in his or her library book.

LESSON 35

Phonics/Spelling

SPELLING EMPHA-SIS: *br* in 2–3 syl-lable words.

VOCABULARY EMPHASIS: Com-munity affairs

MATERIAL: *Time* and *Newsweek*, other magazines

HOMEWORK: Stu-dents use words they choose to spell in sentences.

Composition

PREWRITING: Using student responses, develop a paragraph about movies.

WRITING ASSIGNMENT: Write at least one paragraph about any movie you select.

PROOFREADING THRUST: *Capitalize* the first and impor-tant words in titles.

Study Skills

THEME: Dwellings

MATERIAL: Fiction books

READING ASSIGN-MENT: Locate pic-tures or written pas-sages about dwellings.

WRITING ASSIGN-MENT: Write a detailed description of the dwelling pic-tured or described.

Recreational Reading

PRONOUNS: During each conference, ask the student to locate and discusss different *pronouns* in his or her library book.

LESSON 36

Phonics/Spelling

SPELLING EMPHA-SIS: *pl* in 2–3 syllable words

VOCABULARY EMPHASIS: Employment

MATERIAL: *Time* and *Newsweek*, other magazines

HOMEWORK: Students use words they choose to spell in sentences.

Composition

PREWRITING: Write sentences on the chalkboard volunteered by students about different pets.

WRITING ASSIGNMENT: Write a paragraph about each pet.

PROOFREADING THRUST: *Indent* to begin a new paragraph.

HOMEWORK: Assign pages concerning paragraph development in the textbook.

Study Skills

THEME: Politicians

MATERIAL: Newspapers

READING ASSIGN-MENT: Locate pictures that show politicians. Read the captions. Cut the caption from the picture. Exchange with another student.

WRITING ASSIGN-MENT: Write what you think the caption should be; compare.

Recreational Reading

PRONOUNS: During each conference, ask the student to locate and discuss different *pronouns* in his or her library book.

LESSON 37

Phonics/Spelling

SPELLING EMPHA-SIS: *al* in 2–3 syllable words

VOCABULARY EMPHASIS: Safety

MATERIAL: Newspapers

HOMEWORK: Students use words they choose to spell in sentences.

Composition

PREWRITING: Discuss holidays and write phrases volunteered by the students on the chalkboard.

WRITING ASSIGNMENT: Write paragraphs about at least two holidays.

PROOFREADING THRUST: *Indent* to show paragraphs and include at least one *pronoun* in a sentence.

HOMEWORK: Write a paragraph about another holiday. Draw an illustration.

Study Skills

THEME: Products/crops

MATERIAL: Maps that show crops and/or manufacturing products in an area

READING ASSIGN-MENT: Read the map key to locate information about the crops/products.

WRITING ASSIGN-MENT: Write a list of products.

Recreational Reading

PRONOUNS: During each conference, ask the student to locate and discuss different *pronouns* in his or her library book.

LESSON 38

Phonics/Spelling

SPELLING EMPHA-SIS: *ck* in 2–3 sylla-ble words

VOCABULARY EMPHASIS: Pollu-tion

MATERIAL: News-papers

HOMEWORK: Stu-dents use words they choose to spell in sentences.

Composition

PREWRITING: Discuss "A day in my life."

WRITING ASSIGNMENT: Organize parts of the day in paragraphs. Change paragraphs to show different parts of your day.

PROOFREADING THRUST: Mark *commas* to separate words in a series.

NOTE: This is a two-day time-lapse writing assignment.

Study Skills

THEME: Machines

MATERIAL: Maga-zines

READING ASSIGN-MENT: Locate pic-tures of machines.

WRITING ASSIGN-MENT: Write a list of the machines. Classify the machines by type, use, color, size, etc. (Student chooses classification.)

Recreational Reading

PRONOUNS: During each conference, ask the student to locate and discuss *pronouns* in his or her library book.

LESSON 39

Phonics/Spelling

SPELLING EMPHA-SIS: Vowel cluster *ee* in at least one word in each sen-tence

VOCABULARY EMPHASIS: Busi-ness

MATERIAL: News-papers

HOMEWORK: Make a list of different names of medicines at home. Underline each vowel cluster.

Composition

PREWRITING: Discuss para-graph divisions.

WRITING ASSIGNMENT: Con-tinue writing about "a day in my life." Complete the paper today.

PROOFREADING THRUST: *Indention* of paragraphs and use of *commas* to separate words in a series.

Study Skills

THEME: Machines

MATERIAL: Social studies textbooks

READING ASSIGN-MENT: Locate pic-tures and/or descrip-tions of machines no longer in use.

WRITING ASSIGN-MENT: Make a list of machines and tell why you think they are no longer used.

Recreational Reading

PRONOUNS: During each conference, ask the student to locate and discuss different *pronouns* in his or her library book.

LESSON 40

Phonics/Spelling

SPELLING EMPHA-
SIS: Vowel cluster
ea in at least one
word in each sen-
tence. Or Chart
Review Test

VOCABULARY
EMPHASIS:
Hobbies

MATERIAL: News-
papers

HOMEWORK: Ask a
member of your
family to say words
to you. Write the
words. Underline
any vowel clusters.

Composition

PREWRITING: Free choice topics. Or Sharing Day

WRITING ASSIGNMENT: Write
paragraphs about a topic of your
selection.

PROOFREADING THRUST:
Indent to show change in paragraphs, and underline *topic sentence* in each paragraph.

Study Skills

THEME: Machines

MATERIAL: Science
textbooks

READING ASSIGN-
MENT: Locate pic-
tures and words con-
cerning scientists
using machines.

WRITING ASSIGN-
MENT: Write how
the machines help
the scientists in their
work.

Recreational Reading

PRONOUNS: During
each conference,
ask the student to
locate and discuss
different *pronouns*
in his or her library
book.

PHASE 3—GENERAL PHASE—LESSONS 41–100

LESSON 41

Phonics/Spelling

SPELLING EMPHA-
SIS: *i*

VOCABULARY
EMPHASIS:
Editorials

MATERIAL: *Time,
Newsweek,* or other
magazines

HOMEWORK: Test
with someone at
home. Write sen-
tences including
words about medi-
cine.

Composition

CYCLE 6: WRITING
DIALOGUE

PREWRITING: Discuss *frogs.*
Teacher writes key words and
phrases from students concerning what they know about frogs.

WRITING ASSIGNMENT: Write
dialogue giving information
about a frog.

PROOFREADING THRUST: Use
adjectives to show shades of
color.

Study Skills

CYCLE 6: LOCAT-
ING SPECIFIC
WORDS

KNOWLEDGE
AREA: Parts of the
body

MATERIAL: Music
textbooks

READING/WRITING
FOCUS: Read to
locate and list words
pertaining specifi-
cally to body parts in
music lyrics.

Recreational Reading

CYCLE 6: DIA-
LOGUE Identify
*elements of punc-
tuation* and *content
of dialogues* found
in library books.

LESSON 42

Phonics/Spelling

SPELLING EMPHA-
SIS: *e*

VOCABULARY
EMPHASIS:
Medicine

MATERIAL: News-
papers

HOMEWORK: Use a
spelling textbook to
locate any words
associated directly
or indirectly with
medicine. Under-
line any that begin
with *e*.

Composition

PREWRITING: Discuss a conversation with a frog. Write dialogue on the chalkboard.

WRITING ASSIGNMENT: Write
about a conversation with a
frog.

PROOFREADING THRUST:
Check use of *quotation marks*.

Study Skills

KNOWLEDGE
AREA: Parts of the
body

MATERIAL: Health/
science textbooks

READING/WRITING
FOCUS: Read to
locate names and
functions of parts of
the body. Write
body parts and at
least one function of
each.

Recreational Reading

DIALOGUE: Identify
*elements of punc-
tuation* and *content
of dialogues* found
in library books.

LESSON 43

Phonics/Spelling

SPELLING EMPHA-
SIS: *a*

VOCABULARY
EMPHASIS:
Conservation

MATERIAL: News-
papers

HOMEWORK: Test
with someone at
home. Write a
short paragraph
using some of the
spelling words from
today and/or 2–3
days back in your
notebook or folder.

Composition

PREWRITING: Discuss being
lost.

WRITING ASSIGNMENT: Write
about being lost from parents or
being lost on a trip with your
parents. Include conversation.

PROOFREADING THRUST:
Include words that tell about
time.

HOMEWORK: Language book—
assignments related to dialogue.

Study Skills

KNOWLEDGE
AREA: Parts of the
body

MATERIAL: Maga-
zines

READING/WRITING
FOCUS: Find prod-
ucts in magazines
that are for the care
of the body. Write
whether the prod-
ucts are useful to
you, including why
or why not.

Recreational Reading

DIALOGUE: Identify
*elements of punc-
tuation* and *content
of dialogues* found
in library books.

119

LESSON 44

Phonics/Spelling

SPELLING EMPHA-
SIS: *o*
VOCABULARY
EMPHASIS:
Energy
MATERIAL: News-
papers
HOMEWORK: Test
your list with some-
one at home.
Check together.
Find a product in
your house with *o*
in the name. List
any words contain-
ing *o* on the label.

Composition

PREWRITING: Discuss "scary
things."
WRITING ASSIGNMENT: Write
about a real or imaginary experience with a scary thing.
Include some conversation.
PROOFREADING THRUST: Use
a *comma* to separate the spoken
words from the unspoken parts
of the sentences.

Study Skills

KNOWLEDGE
AREA: Measure-
ment
MATERIAL: Mathe-
matics textbooks
READING/WRITING
FOCUS: Read to
find and list words
about measurement,
especially related to
the metric system.
Classify the words
according to length,
weight, or volume.

Recreational Reading

DIALOGUE: Identify
*elements of punc-
tuation* and *content
of dialogues* found
in library books.

LESSON 45

Phonics/Spelling

SPELLING EMPHA-
SIS: *oo*
VOCABULARY
EMPHASIS:
Advertisements
MATERIAL: News-
paper
HOMEWORK: Test
with a parent.
Check together.
Use a spelling book
to find other *oo*
words to learn at
home.

Composition

PREWRITING: Discuss talking
trees in a magic forest.
WRITING ASSIGNMENT: Write
the conversation you might
have with talking trees in a
magic forest.
PROOFREADING THRUST:
Descriptive words.
HOMEWORK: Language book—
pages related to quotation
marks.

Study Skills

KNOWLEDGE
AREA: Measure-
ment
MATERIAL: Food
labels, packages, or
advertisements in
food section of news-
papers
READING/WRITING
FOCUS: Find words
relating to measure-
ment. Make a list of
measurement words,
including abbrevia-
tions.

Recreational Reading

DIALOGUE: Identify
*elements of punc-
tuation* and *content
of dialogues* found
in library books.

LESSON 46

Phonics/Spelling

SPELLING EMPHA-SIS: *oa*

VOCABULARY EMPHASIS: Advertisements

MATERIAL: *Time, Newsweek*, or other magazines

HOMEWORK: Test with parent. Use your spelling text-book to find some *oa* words to learn. Use these words in sentences.

Composition

PREWRITING: Discuss what you would say to someone from another planet.

WRITING ASSIGNMENT: Create a situation in which you must have a conversation with a being from another planet.

PROOFREADING THRUST: Change of paragraph to show change of speaker.

Study Skills

KNOWLEDGE AREA: Measure-ment

MATERIAL: Food packages

READING/WRITING FOCUS: Locate and write standard mea-surement and corre-sponding metric measurement of products in chart form.

HOMEWORK: Find some measurement words on items at home.

Recreational Reading

DIALOGUE: Identify *elements of punc-tuation* and *content of dialogues* found in library books.

LESSON 47

Phonics/Spelling

SPELLING EMPHA-SIS: *u*

VOCABULARY EMPHASIS: Com-puters

MATERIAL: *Time, Newsweek*, or other magazines

HOMEWORK: Use a dictionary to find the meanings of two or three words the teacher chooses.

Composition

PREWRITING: Discuss "The Giant Pumpkin."

WRITING ASSIGNMENT: Write information related to pump-kins—growth, uses, etc.

PROOFREADING THRUST: Include words to denote *degrees in size*.

Study Skills

CYCLE 7: UNDER-STANDING A MAP KEY

KNOWLEDGE AREA: Land forms

MATERIAL: Social studies textbook

READING/WRITING FOCUS: Read map key in a social stud-ies book. Copy key and *write explana-tions* of what the map tells you about land forms.

Recreational Reading

DIALOGUE: Identify *elements of punc-tuation* and *content of dialogues* found in library books.

LESSON 48

Phonics/Spelling

SPELLING EMPHA-SIS: *y*

VOCABULARY EMPHASIS: Machines

MATERIAL: Newspaper

HOMEWORK: Test with a parent. Write sentences or paragraphs using words teacher chooses from the chart.

Composition

PREWRITING: Continue discussion of "The Giant Pumpkin."

WRITING ASSIGNMENT: Write an imaginary story with dialogue in the story.

PROOFREADING THRUST: *Indent* to show a change in speaker in dialogue.

HOMEWORK: Language textbook—related exercises using quotation marks.

Study Skills

KNOWLEDGE AREA: Land forms

MATERIAL: Encyclopedia or social studies textbook

READING/WRITING FOCUS: Find any map that shows land forms. *Write* as many *facts* as you can from the map and map key information.

Recreational Reading

DIALOGUE: Identify *elements of punctuation* and *content of dialogues* found in library books.

LESSON 49

Phonics/Spelling

SPELLING EMPHA-SIS: *ai*

VOCABULARY EMPHASIS: Art

MATERIAL: Newspaper

HOMEWORK: Test with parent. Draw and/or write an advertisement of your own using an *H* word.

Composition

PREWRITING: Discuss falling colored leaves.

WRITING ASSIGNMENT: Write sentences about different kinds, colors, reasons for falling, etc.

PROOFREADING THRUST: Include a sentence beginning with "When . ."

HOMEWORK: At home, find several different fallen leaves. Write a sentence to describe each leaf.

Study Skills

KNOWLEDGE AREA: Land forms

MATERIAL: Paper and crayons

READING/WRITING FOCUS: Draw an outline of an imaginary state. Design key to show different land forms in your state. Color in land forms to relate to your key.

Recreational Reading

DIALOGUE: Identify *elements of punctuation* and *content of dialogues* found in library books.

LESSON 50

Phonics/Spelling

SPELLING EMPHA-SIS: *aw*

VOCABULARY EMPHASIS: Music. Or Chart Review Day

MATERIAL: Newspaper

HOMEWORK: Test with a parent. List any song titles you can that have a *j* in the title.

Composition

PREWRITING: Continue discussing falling colored leaves. Or Sharing Day

WRITING ASSIGNMENT: Write a dialogue between leaves and people.

PROOFREADING THRUST: Use *correct elements of direct quotations.*

Study Skills

CYCLE 8: DEVELOPING LISTENING SKILLS: KNOWLEDGE AREA: Television personalities

MATERIAL: T.V. guide or other material containing information about television personalities

READING/WRITING FOCUS: Teacher reads article about a television personality. Teacher asks factual questions based on the article. Students write answers. Check together to assess accuracy.

HOMEWORK: Ask a parent to read an article aloud and ask factual questions.

Recreational Reading

DIALOGUE: Identify *elements of punctuation* and *content of dialogues* found in library books.

LESSON 51

Phonics/Spelling

SPELLING EMPHASIS: *qu*

VOCABULARY EMPHASIS: Issues

MATERIAL: Newspaper

HOMEWORK: Test at home. Take a list of *qu* words on chart to alphabetize at home.

Composition

CYCLE 7: WRITING SHORT STORIES

PREWRITING: Discuss forest fire!

WRITING ASSIGNMENT: Write sentences of factual information.

PROOFREADING THRUST: Use words to show *time change*.

Study Skills

KNOWLEDGE AREA: Story settings

MATERIAL: Short story collection or other source

READING/WRITING FOCUS: Teacher reads short story. Students listen, then write a list of settings in the story.

Recreational Reading

CYCLE 7: NOUNS Locate *common and proper nouns* in library books.

LESSON 52

Phonics/Spelling

SPELLING EMPHASIS: *er*

VOCABULARY EMPHASIS: Issues

MATERIAL: *Time*, *Newsweek*, or other magazines

HOMEWORK: Write a paragraph about music. Use any words in your notebook you can.

Composition

PREWRITING: Continue discussion of forest fire! Discuss elements of writing short stories.

WRITING ASSIGNMENT: Write a short creative story about a forest fire.

PROOFREADING THRUST: Use *!* to show excitement.

Study Skills

KNOWLEDGE AREA: Famous people

MATERIAL: Library book about a famous person

READING/WRITING FOCUS: Teacher reads his or her choice of material. Student designs questions (with answers) to ask a partner—check each.

Recreational Reading

NOUNS: Locate *common and proper nouns* in library books.

LESSON 53

Phonics/Spelling

SPELLING EMPHASIS: *in*

VOCABULARY EMPHASIS: National events

MATERIAL: *Time, Newsweek,* or other magazines

HOMEWORK: Find words containing *in* in your spelling textbook that you can learn to spell. Test with a parent.

Composition

PREWRITING: Discuss flocks of birds.

WRITING ASSIGNMENT: Write an introductory paragraph for a short story about a flock of *birds*. (2-day time-lapse writing)

PROOFREADING THRUST: Include *contractions*.

HOMEWORK: Use language textbook to practice use of subject/verb agreement.

Study Skills

CYCLE 9: USING A TIME LINE

KNOWLEDGE AREA: Autobiographical time line

MATERIAL: Teacher-designed autobiographical time line on board

READING/WRITING FOCUS: Discuss example on board. Students design their own autobiographical time line.

Recreational Reading

NOUNS: Locate *common and proper nouns* in library books.

LESSON 54

Phonics/Spelling

SPELLING EMPHASIS: *ur*

VOCABULARY EMPHASIS: Comics

MATERIAL: Newspaper

HOMEWORK: Test with parent. Make a list of any music groups that have *s* in their name.

Composition

PREWRITING: Continue discussion of flocks of birds.

WRITING ASSIGNMENT: Complete a short story begun yesterday in Lesson 53.

PROOFREADING THRUST: Begin one sentence with "If . . ."

HOMEWORK: Continue subject/verb agreement by assigning exercises in language textbook.

Study Skills

KNOWLEDGE AREA: Presidents

MATERIAL: Encyclopedia

READING/WRITING FOCUS: Read about one specific president. Select main dates in his life and arrange on a time line. (Teacher may assign groups to work together on specific presidents.) Day 1 of a 2-day assignment.

Recreational Reading

NOUNS: Locate *common and proper nouns* in library books.

LESSON 55

Phonics/Spelling

SPELLING EMPHA-
SIS: *ir*

VOCABULARY
EMPHASIS:
Nature

MATERIAL: News-
paper

HOMEWORK: Write
a short paragraph
about your favorite
food word on the
list.

Composition

PREWRITING: Discuss great
inventions.

WRITING ASSIGNMENT: Write
information about inventions
you think are important. Tell
how and/or why.

PROOFREADING THRUST:
Include *verbs* in the past tense.

HOMEWORK: Use language
textbook to practice use of pres-
ent/past tense of verbs.

Study Skills

KNOWLEDGE
AREA: Presidents

MATERIAL: None (or
use encyclopedia
from previous lesson)

READING/WRITING
FOCUS: Present
and discuss time
lines.

Recreational Reading

NOUNS: Locate *com-
mon and proper
nouns* in library
books.

LESSON 56

Phonics/Spelling

SPELLING EMPHA-
SIS: *er*

VOCABULARY
EMPHASIS: Food

MATERIAL: News-
paper

HOMEWORK: Test
with a parent. Look
on one food label at
home. List the *d*,
D words on the
label.

Composition

PREWRITING: Continue discussion of great inventions.

WRITING ASSIGNMENT: Write
a story including advantages of
the inventions.

PROOFREADING THRUST:
Verbs.

HOMEWORK: Draw a scene
from your story, or draw a diagram to explain your invention.

Study Skills

CYCLE 10: INTER-
PRETING GRAPHS

KNOWLEDGE
AREA: Economy (or
varies with each
graph)

MATERIAL: Mathe-
matics textbook

READING/WRITING
FOCUS: Students
use same graph in a
textbook to obtain
the basic information
provided by the
graph. Write the
information found.

Recreational Reading

NOUNS: Locate *com-
mon and proper
nouns* in library
books.

LESSON 57

Phonics/Spelling

SPELLING EMPHA-
SIS: *an*
VOCABULARY
EMPHASIS:
Accidents
MATERIAL: News-
papers
HOMEWORK: Find
an words in your
spelling textbook to
study and test with
a parent.

Composition

PREWRITING: Discuss "slick and
slimy."
WRITING ASSIGNMENT: Write
your version of "slick and
slimy."
PROOFREADING THRUST:
Include one *prepositional
phrase* to show position. Examples: *on the floor, in the pan*.
HOMEWORK: Use any material
(language textbook, etc.) to
locate prepositional phrases.

Study Skills

KNOWLEDGE
AREA: Economy (or
varies with each
graph)
MATERIAL: Social
studies textbook or
teacher-designed
graph worksheet
READING/WRITING
FOCUS: Students
may locate any
graph, or teacher
may indicate one.
Write a summary in
your own words of
what information is
included in graph.
How is the graph
useful in giving
information?

Recreational Reading

NOUNS: Locate *com-
mon and proper
nouns* in library
books.

LESSON 58

Phonics/Spelling

SPELLING EMPHASIS: *l, L*

VOCABULARY EMPHASIS: Television

MATERIAL: *Time, Newsweek*, or other magazines

Composition

PREWRITING: Continue discussion of "slick and slimy."

WRITING ASSIGNMENT: Write an imaginary story using the topic words, "slick and slimy."

PROOFREADING THRUST: Include a *possessive ('s) form*.

Study Skills

KNOWLEDGE AREA: Economy (or varies with each graph)

MATERIAL: Encyclopedia.

READING/WRITING FOCUS: Students choose any *graph*. Write a description of the information given. Compare any two facts on the graph.

Recreational Reading

NOUNS: Locate *common and proper nouns* in library books.

LESSON 59

Phonics/Spelling

SPELLING EMPHASIS: *es*

VOCABULARY EMPHASIS: Happy things

MATERIAL: *Time, Newsweek*, or other magazines

HOMEWORK: Write a short paragraph using some of chart words to tell of at least one "happy thing."

Composition

PREWRITING: Discuss "a prehistoric adventure."

WRITING ASSIGNMENT: Locate and write factual information about life in prehistoric times.

PROOFREADING THRUST: Use adverbs *slowly, quickly* and/or other *ly* adverbs.

HOMEWORK: Use language textbook to assign homework on adverbs.

Study Skills

CYCLE 11: LOCATING DETAILS

KNOWLEDGE AREA: Plants

MATERIAL: Science textbook

READING/WRITING FOCUS: Read to *locate parts* of plants. List and tell what each basic part does.

Recreational Reading

NOUNS: Locate *common and proper nouns* in library books.

LESSON 60

Phonics/Spelling

SPELLING EMPHA-
  SIS: *ss*
VOCABULARY
  EMPHASIS: Sad
  things. Or Chart
  Review Test
MATERIAL: News-
  paper
HOMEWORK: Test
  with a parent.
  Write about one
  sad thing you have
  experienced.

Composition

PREWRITING: Continue discussion of a prehistoric adventure.
  Or Sharing Day
WRITING ASSIGNMENT: Write
  an imaginary story about the
  topic.
PROOFREADING THRUST: Use
  at least one *verb* of future tense.
HOMEWORK: Language text-
  book or worksheet on adverbs,
  use of, etc.

Study Skills

KNOWLEDGE
  AREA: Plants
MATERIAL: Encyclo-
  pedia
READING/WRITING
  FOCUS: Students
  locate a plant in the
  encyclopedia. Read
  to find instructions
  about the care of a
  plant. Write the
  important details
  about the care of this
  plant.

Recreational Reading

NOUNS: Locate *com-
  mon and proper
  nouns* in library
  books.

LESSON 61

Phonics/Spelling

CYCLE 2: ACADEMIC VOCABULARY WITH STRUCTURAL EMPHASIS

STRUCTURAL EMPHASIS: Abbreviations

VOCABULARY EMPHASIS: Mathematics words, time (clock and calendar)

WRITING: Write a paragraph using words of time. Circle the ones you will spell. Test and file.

HOMEWORK: Write sentences using words to tell the time you get up, eat dinner, go to bed, etc.

Composition

CYCLE 8: WRITING LETTERS

PREWRITING: Discuss invitations to parties. Outline a model letter on chalkboard.

WRITING ASSIGNMENT: Write an invitation to a party in letter form. (Draw a name of a classmate to invite.)

PROOFREADING THRUST: Check *comma* after greeting and closing.

Study Skills

KNOWLEDGE AREA: Plants

MATERIAL: Health textbook

READING/WRITING FOCUS: Read to find out about plants that are important to your health. How are they important? List the plant and tell why it is important. (E.g., citrus fruits have vitamin C.)

Recreational Reading

CYCLE 8: CHARACTERS Identify *descriptions of characters*.

LESSON 62

Phonics/Spelling

STRUCTURAL EMPHASIS: Suffix, *ment*

VOCABULARY EMPHASIS: Mathematics words, money

WRITING: Write a paragraph using words referring to money. Circle the words you will test on.

HOMEWORK: Find items with prices marked on them at home. Write out the prices using words, no numbers.

Composition

PREWRITING: Discuss replies to invitations. Deliver invitations written the previous lesson to classmate.

WRITING ASSIGNMENT: Write a reply in letter form to the invitation.

PROOFREADING THRUST: Use *commas* to separate city, state, day, and year.

Study Skills

KNOWLEDGE AREA: Inventions

MATERIAL: Social studies textbook

READING/WRITING FOCUS: Read to find information about inventions. List invention, inventor, date.

Recreational Reading

CHARACTERS: Identify *descriptions of characters*.

131

LESSON 63

Phonics/Spelling

STRUCTURAL EMPHASIS: Division of words into syllables.

VOCABULARY EMPHASIS: Mathematics words, geometry

WRITING: Write a paragraph using words from the chart.

HOMEWORK: Find and list objects in your home that illustrate geometric shapes. Examples: *square*, *table*, *room*. Test on word list, too.

Composition

PREWRITING: Discuss kinds of letters written to adults.

WRITING ASSIGNMENT: Write a letter to an adult.

PROOFREADING THRUST: Use a *period* after abbreviated titles.

HOMEWORK: Assign pages in language textbook on letter forms and envelopes.

Study Skills

KNOWLEDGE AREA: Inventions

MATERIAL: Encyclopedia

READING/WRITING FOCUS: Read to find an invention or inventor in the encyclopedia from the list in Lesson 62. Write important *details* from the information read.

Recreational Reading

CHARACTERS: Identify *descriptions of characters*.

LESSON 64

Phonics/Spelling

STRUCTURAL EMPHASIS: Various prefixes used in metric system such as *milli, centi*

VOCABULARY EMPHASIS: Measurement (metric and standard)

WRITING: Write a paragraph using words from the chart.

HOMEWORK: Look on a food label or package to find any measurement words. Make a list. Test on word list.

Composition

PREWRITING: Discuss letters written to thank someone for a gift.

WRITING ASSIGNMENT: Write a letter to thank someone for a gift you have received.

PROOFREADING THRUST: *Punctuation* in a friendly letter.

Study Skills

KNOWLEDGE AREA: Inventions

MATERIAL: Magazines

READING/WRITING FOCUS: Read to find pictures (and/or descriptions) of inventions you use. Write about how your life would be different if you didn't have this invention.

Recreational Reading

CHARACTERS: Identify *descriptions of characters*.

LESSON 65

Phonics/Spelling

STRUCTURAL EMPHASIS: Suffix, *ty*.

VOCABULARY EMPHASIS: Mathematics words (numbers)

WRITING: Use number words from the chart in a paragraph.

HOMEWORK: Write, in sentences, number facts about your family. Use words to tell numbers. Example: We have four in my family. My father is thirty-two.

Composition

PREWRITING: Discuss possible inclusions in a letter about a school function.

WRITING ASSIGNMENT: Write a letter to give information to your parents about any school event.

PROOFREADING THRUST: Use of a *contraction*.

HOMEWORK: Take the letter home; return it the next day with parent's signature; file the letter.

Study Skills

CYCLE 12: UNDERSTANDING SYMBOLS

KNOWLEDGE AREA: Mathematical symbols

MATERIAL: Mathematics textbook

READING/WRITING FOCUS: Read in mathematics textbook to recognize *symbols* (not words). Make a list of the symbols and write the word or words for the symbol. Example: L = angle, % = percent, + = plus.

Recreational Reading

CHARACTERS: Identify *descriptions of characters*.

LESSON 66

Phonics/Spelling

STRUCTURAL EMPHASIS: Prefix, *un*

VOCABULARY EMPHASIS: Science words (weather)

WRITING: Use some weather words from the chart in a paragraph.

HOMEWORK: Listen to the weather news. Write down all weather words you can. Check spelling in dictionary.

Composition

PREWRITING: Discuss letters to the editor.

WRITING ASSIGNMENT: Write a letter to an editor.

PROOFREADING THRUST: Do not begin a sentence with *and*.

Study Skills

KNOWLEDGE AREA: Punctuation symbols

MATERIAL: Language textbook

READING/WRITING FOCUS: Look for the punctuation symbols. List, tell what each means, and use each in a sentence. Example: Quotation marks signify direct words spoken. He said, "Let's go."

Recreational Reading

CHARACTERS: Identify *descriptions of characters.*

LESSON 67

Phonics/Spelling

STRUCTURAL EMPHASIS: Nouns which form plurals with -s

VOCABULARY EMPHASIS: Science words (plants)

WRITING: Write sentences or paragraph using chart words. Choose several. Study, test, check, file.

HOMEWORK: Make a list of the names of any plants in or around your home. Put in alphabetical order.

Composition

PREWRITING: Discuss contents of a letter to a famous person.

WRITING ASSIGNMENT: Write a letter to a famous person.

PROOFREADING THRUST: Include an *interrogative sentence* and *question mark*.

Study Skills

KNOWLEDGE AREA: Math and punctuation symbols

MATERIAL: Newspaper

READING/WRITING FOCUS: Use newspaper for a "scavenger hunt." Teacher gives out list of *symbols* to search for in newspaper. (Cut out as you find and paste on sheet.) Timed activity. Example of items on list:
1. circle
2. period
3. question mark
4. square
5. decimal number
6. number over 50
7. quotation marks
8. triangle
9. fraction
10. square

(Student may circle or underline instead of cutting and pasting.)

Recreational Reading

CHARACTERS: Identify *descriptions of characters*.

LESSON 68

Phonics/Spelling

STRUCTURAL EMPHASIS: Suffix, *ish*

VOCABULARY EMPHASIS: Science words (animals)

WRITING: Write a paragraph or sentences using chart words. List, test, check, file.

HOMEWORK: Draw a picture of any animal on the chart. Write facts about the animal.

Composition

PREWRITING: Discuss contents of a letter to the school cafeteria manager.

WRITING ASSIGNMENT: Write a letter emphasizing positive aspects of the cafeteria. Have more than one paragraph in the letter.

PROOFREADING THRUST: *Indent* to show new paragraphs.

Study Skills

KNOWLEDGE AREA: Letter symbols

MATERIAL: Magazines

READING/WRITING FOCUS: Read to find words with the long *e* sound spelled with different letters. List the words. Underline letters that *symbolize* the long *e* sound.

Recreational Reading

CHARACTERS: Identify *descriptions of characters.*

LESSON 69

Phonics/Spelling

STRUCTURAL EMPHASIS: Suffix, *ist*

VOCABULARY EMPHASIS: Science words (medicine)

WRITING: Write a paragraph using chart words. Test.

HOMEWORK: With a parent, read a medicine label or package at home. List any words you had trouble pronouncing. Look up the respelling in a dictionary.

Composition

PREWRITING: Discuss a letter to the principal.

WRITING ASSIGNMENT: Write a 3-paragraph letter to the principal. Each paragraph should be about a different topic, and all topics should refer to the school.

PROOFREADING THRUST: Use a *period* after abbreviations and use a *comma* after greeting and closing of letter.

Study Skills

KNOWLEDGE AREA: Pronunciation symbols

MATERIAL: Spelling textbook

READING/WRITING FOCUS: Use the pronunciation key in textbook to find the symbols and key words to find out how to *write your name phonetically*.

Recreational Reading

CHARACTERS: Identify *descriptions of characters*.

LESSON 70

Phonics/Spelling

STRUCTURAL
  EMPHASIS: Pre-
  fix, *in*
VOCABULARY
  EMPHASIS: Sci-
  ence words (space)
WRITING: Write a
  paragraph. Test. Or
  Chart Review Test
HOMEWORK: Write
  a short creative
  story using some
  chart space words.

Composition

PREWRITING: Discuss possible
  contents in a letter written
  while away from home. Or
  Sharing Day
WRITING ASSIGNMENT: Pre-
  tend you are visiting away from
  home. Write a letter to your
  family.
PROOFREADING THRUST:
  Check *verbs* in your sentences.

Study Skills

KNOWLEDGE
  AREA: Pronuncia-
  tion symbols
MATERIAL: Diction-
  aries and fiction book
READING/WRITING
  FOCUS: Find
  "everyday" words in
  a fiction book. Find
  the respellings in a
  dictionary. Write
  only the respellings
  for a partner.
  Exchange to see if
  partner can write the
  actual word from the
  respelling.

Recreational Reading

CHARACTERS:
  Identify *descrip-
  tions of characters.*

139

LESSON 71

Phonics/Spelling

STRUCTURAL
EMPHASIS: Suffix,
tion
VOCABULARY
EMPHASIS: Geog-
raphy words (land
types)
WRITING: Write a
paragraph. Test.
HOMEWORK: Find
any chart words
you can in your
social studies book.
List, tell the page,
and define.

Composition

CYCLE 9: WRITING POETRY
PREWRITING: Discuss spaghetti.
WRITING ASSIGNMENT: Write
a descriptive paragraph about
spaghetti. Include descriptive
words.
PROOFREADING THRUST:
Begin one sentence with *when*.

Study Skills

CYCLE 12: MAP
READING: Inter-
preting information
on a map.
KNOWLEDGE
AREA: Our state
MATERIAL: Newspa-
per weather map
READING/WRITING
FOCUS: Read the
explanation of the
weather map sym-
bols, write facts
about the state's
weather from infor-
mation given on the
map and map key.

Recreational Reading

CYCLE 9: APOS-
TROPHES Identify
*apostrophes in con-
tractions and pos-
sessives* in library
book.

LESSON 72

Phonics/Spelling

STRUCTURAL
EMPHASIS: Suffix,
ness
VOCABULARY
EMPHASIS: Geog-
raphy words (maps)
WRITING: Write a
paragraph. Check
list and test.
HOMEWORK: Draw
a simple map to
show any terms you
listed on your
chart.

Composition

PREWRITING: Continue discussion of spaghetti. Discuss
poetry. Show *cinquain* form on
board. Write a poem together
about "spaghetti."

WRITING ASSIGNMENT: Write
a cinquain poem about your
favorite food or any topic you
choose.

PROOFREADING THRUST:
Check your cinquain form:
1st line—theme, 1 word.
2nd line—2 describing words.
3rd line—3 action words.
4th line—4 words expressing feelings about theme word.
5th line—1 word, a synonym for
theme word.

Study Skills

KNOWLEDGE
AREA: Our state
MATERIAL: State
road map
READING/WRITING
FOCUS: Use map to
name features of our
state. Write any facts
you can using only
the map. Example:
Raleigh is the capi-
tal.

Recreational Reading

Identify *apostrophes
in contractions and
possessives* in
library book.

LESSON 73

Phonics/Spelling

STRUCTURAL EMPHASIS: Prefix, *inter*

VOCABULARY EMPHASIS: Geography words (cities and states)

WRITING: Write a paragraph using some chart words. Make a test list. Test, check, file.

HOMEWORK: Write a story about a trip you would like to take to one city on the chart.

Composition

PREWRITING: Discuss nature. Discuss poetry form Haiku.

WRITING ASSIGNMENT: Write a Haiku about a topic you choose.

PROOFREADING THRUST: Correct Haiku form.
5 syllables—1st line,
7 syllables—2nd line,
5 syllables—3rd line.

HOMEWORK: Give each student a newspaper page. At home underline any *ing* verbs you find.

Study Skills

KNOWLEDGE AREA: Our state

MATERIAL: U.S. map (in social studies textbook)

READING/WRITING FOCUS: Use the map to write as many facts as you can about our state. Relate to size, bordering states, etc. Example: Our state is bordered by ——
—, ——, ——, and ——.

Recreational Reading

Identify *apostrophes in contractions and possessives* in library book.

LESSON 74

Phonics/Spelling

STRUCTURAL EMPHASIS: Plural form of nouns

VOCABULARY EMPHASIS: Geography words (bodies of water)

WRITING: Write a paragraph. Make a test list. Test, check, file.

HOMEWORK: At home with your family, make a list of different kinds of bodies of water.

Composition

PREWRITING TOPIC: Discuss "country life." Discuss free verse, no rhyme or meter.

WRITING ASSIGNMENT: Write a poem in free verse about "country life."

PROOFREADING THRUST: *Capitalize* each line of poetry.

Study Skills

CYCLE 14: UNDER- STANDING ADVERTISED INFORMATION

KNOWLEDGE AREA: Buying and selling

MATERIAL: Newspaper, classified ads

READING/WRITING FOCUS: Read the classified ads to find an article for sale you would like to buy. Cut out the ad. Write your own ad to advertise something that you could sell.

Recreational Reading

Identify *apostrophes in contractions and possessives* in library book.

LESSON 75

Phonics/Spelling

STRUCTURAL
EMPHASIS: Suffix,
ly
VOCABULARY
EMPHASIS: Geography words (globe)
WRITING: Write a
paragraph using
chart words. Test
list. Test, check,
file.
HOMEWORK:
Select a spot on the
globe. Write about
"your visit" to that
place.

Composition

PREWRITING: Discuss humor,
nonsense. Discuss poetry form,
limericks.
WRITING ASSIGNMENT: Write
a limerick about topic you
choose.
PROOFREADING THRUST:
Limerick—rhyme and rhythm.

Study Skills

KNOWLEDGE
AREA: Real estate
MATERIAL: Newspaper, real estate ads
READING/WRITING
FOCUS: Choose an
apartment to rent.
Explain the features
of the apartment that
appeal to you. (Some
will be abbreviations.)

Recreational Reading

Identify *apostrophes
in contractions and
possessives* in
library book.

LESSON 76

Phonics/Spelling

STRUCTURAL
EMPHASIS: Silent
letters in words
VOCABULARY
EMPHASIS: History words (important people)
WRITING: Write a
paragraph. Test
list. Test, check,
file.
HOMEWORK: Write
a paragraph about
any famous person.

Composition

PREWRITING: Discuss "footprints in the snow" or "snow
storm." Introduce couplet.
Write one or more couplets on
board with students.
WRITING ASSIGNMENT: Write
couplets.
PROOFREADING THRUST:
Ending words rhyme.

Study Skills

KNOWLEDGE
AREA: Money
MATERIAL: Catalogues, newspapers,
and ads
READING/WRITING
FOCUS: Plan to buy
presents for friends
or family. List presents and costs.

Recreational Reading

Identify *apostrophes
in contractions and
possessives* in
library book.

LESSON 77

Phonics/Spelling

STRUCTURAL EMPHASIS: Silent letters in words

VOCABULARY EMPHASIS: History words (current events)

WRITING ASSIGNMENT: Write a paragraph about a current event, or use chart words.

HOMEWORK: Watch the news to find out about one current event. Write about it in a paragraph.

Composition

PREWRITING: Discuss "A Special Gift."

WRITING ASSIGNMENT: Write a paragraph about a gift you have gotten or given that was "special" in some way.

PROOFREADING THRUST: Use a *past tense verb*.

Study Skills

KNOWLEDGE AREA: Comparative buying

MATERIAL: Catalogue, newspaper ads

READING/WRITING FOCUS: Read ads to find out cost and quality of products. Explain your choice of a product in a paragraph.

Recreational Reading

Identify *apostrophes in contractions and possessives* in library book.

LESSON 78

Phonics/Spelling

STRUCTURAL EMPHASIS: Suffix, *ing*

VOCABULARY EMPHASIS: History words (government)

WRITING ASSIGNMENT: Write a paragraph using some chart words. Test list. Check, file.

HOMEWORK: Write sentences using 3 chart words you did not test yourself on in class.

Composition

PREWRITING: Continue discussion of "A Special Gift." Read some poems to discuss rhythm in poems (meter).

WRITING ASSIGNMENT: Write a poem of 4 or more lines telling of a special gift.

PROOFREADING THRUST: Use *adjectives* to tell about emotions.

Study Skills

KNOWLEDGE AREA: Budgeting money

MATERIAL: Newspapers and catalogues

READING/WRITING FOCUS: You have $2,000 to furnish your apartment. List items you will need to buy and total the cost.

Recreational Reading

Identify *apostrophes in contractions and possessives* in library book.

LESSON 79

Phonics/Spelling

STRUCTURAL EMPHASIS: Prefix, *pre*

VOCABULARY EMPHASIS: History words (important events)

WRITING: Write a paragraph. Test list. Test, check, file.

HOMEWORK: Write a paragraph about an important event in your life.

Composition

PREWRITING: Discuss picture or shape poems. Discuss poems whose shape or form lends to the title or theme of the poem.

WRITING ASSIGNMENT: Write a poem about a topic you choose in a certain shape or picture that helps illustrate your title or subject.

PROOFREADING THRUST: The use of a *simile*.

Study Skills

CYCLE 15: CLASSIFYING

KNOWLEDGE AREA: Budgeting money

MATERIAL: Menu and restaurant ads

READING/WRITING FOCUS: Imagine you take some friends out to eat. Choose an amount you spend. List who eats what (cost of each item). Total the bill and add a tip!

Recreational Reading

Identify *apostrophes in contractions and possessives* in library book.

LESSON 80

Phonics/Spelling

STRUCTURAL EMPHASIS: Prefix, *un*

VOCABULARY EMPHASIS: History words (colonial life)

WRITING: Write a paragraph. Test list. Test, check, file. Or Chart Review Test

HOMEWORK: Draw a picture to show or illustrate any chart words.

Composition

PREWRITING: Discuss "a pet elephant." Read Ogden Nash's "The Leopard," "Hippopotamus," "A Purple Cow," or other humorous poetry. Discuss humorous poetry. Or Sharing Day

WRITING ASSIGNMENT: Write a poem entitled "A Pet ————."

PROOFREADING THRUST: Each line is *capitalized*.

Study Skills

KNOWLEDGE AREA: Construction materials

MATERIAL: Magazines

READING/WRITING FOCUS: Choose a picture and cut it out. Study the picture carefully. *Classify* all items in the picture according to categories you choose. Work with a partner.

Recreational Reading

Identify *apostrophes in contractions and possessives* in library book.

LESSON 81

Phonics/Spelling

STRUCTURAL EMPHASIS: Proper nouns capitalized

VOCABULARY EMPHASIS: Music words (famous musicians, popular or other)

WRITING: Write a paragraph. Test list. Test, check, file.

HOMEWORK: Write a short paragraph about a musician you would like to be. Tell why.

Composition

CYCLE 10: USING PRONOUNS IN SENTENCES

PREWRITING: Define *pronouns*. Write sentences on board to show different kinds of pronouns in use.

WRITING ASSIGNMENT: Use the newspaper. Find sentences using pronouns. Copy each sentence. Underline the pronoun. Then write who the pronoun stands for.

PROOFREADING THRUST: *Pronouns* and *antecedents*.

HOMEWORK: Write sentences using subject pronouns.

Study Skills

KNOWLEDGE AREA: Sports

MATERIAL: Sports section of newspaper

READING/WRITING FOCUS: Make a list of key words from the sports section of a newspaper. Then classify the words into two or more groups.

Recreational Reading

CYCLE 10: PRONOUNS Locate *pronouns and their referents.*

LESSON 82

Phonics/Spelling

STRUCTURAL EMPHASIS: Prefix, *dis*

VOCABULARY EMPHASIS: Music words (terms or forms)

WRITING: Write a paragraph about music you enjoy.

HOMEWORK: When you watch TV tonight, write down different times music is part of the program.

Composition

PREWRITING: Discuss "Slithery Snakes." Write sentences on board; use of pronouns stressed.

WRITING ASSIGNMENT: Write a paragraph entitled "Slithery Snakes."

PROOFREADING THRUST: Use at least one subject *pronoun* in your paper.

Study Skills

KNOWLEDGE AREA: Food

MATERIAL: Newspaper grocery ads

READING/WRITING FOCUS: Read ads to make a list of foods. Group them in a way you choose.

Recreational Reading

PRONOUNS: Locate *pronouns and their referents.*

LESSON 83

Phonics/Spelling

STRUCTURAL EMPHASIS: Suffix, *ful*

VOCABULARY EMPHASIS: Music (popular music— phrases or titles)

WRITING: Write a paragraph or sentence using chart words.

HOMEWORK: Write about a song you like. Tell why.

Composition

PREWRITING: Discuss different occupations. Underline and discuss any examples of "being" verbs in sample sentences on the board.

WRITING: Write sentences about occupations.

PROOFREADING THRUST: Use at least one *being verb* in a sentence.

Study Skills

CYCLE 16: USING CARD CATALOGUE

KNOWLEDGE AREA: Book titles

MATERIAL: File cards for library fiction books

READING/WRITING FOCUS: Teacher introduces title cards and uses. Student makes a *facsimile of a title card* for his or her own book.

Recreational Reading

PRONOUNS: Locate *pronouns and their referents.*

LESSON 84

Phonics/Spelling

STRUCTURAL EMPHASIS: Suffix, *ian*

VOCABULARY EMPHASIS: Music words (instruments)

WRITING: Write a paragraph or sentences about musical instruments.

HOMEWORK: Study spelling of names of different musical instruments.

Composition

PREWRITING: Discuss carnivorous plants. Underline any pronouns in sample sentences on the board.

WRITING ASSIGNMENT: Write a science fiction story about carnivorous plants.

PROOFREADING THRUST: Use at least one *pronoun* in a sentence.

HOMEWORK: Use of pronouns (object, esp.) in language textbook.

Study Skills

KNOWLEDGE AREA: Book topics

MATERIAL: Strips of paper with general topics, card catalogue drawers

READING/WRITING FOCUS: Students are given card catalogue drawer and subject strips which can be found in card catalogue. Find books about your subject. Write the *titles* on the back of the subject strip of paper.

Recreational Reading

PRONOUNS: Locate *pronouns and their referents.*

LESSON 85

Phonics/Spelling

STRUCTURAL EMPHASIS: Plural forms of nouns

VOCABULARY EMPHASIS: Music words (music groups—kinds and/ or specific ones, for example, duet, trio, choir)

WRITING: Write a paragraph. Test list. Test, check, file.

HOMEWORK: Divide the chart words into common and proper nouns.

Composition

PREWRITING: Discuss telephone conversations.

WRITING ASSIGNMENT: Write a telephone conversation. Use the "play" form to show speaker, or use paragraphs and quotation marks.

PROOFREADING THRUST: Use at least one question with proper *punctuation*.

HOMEWORK: Sentences to insert correct pronoun.

Study Skills

KNOWLEDGE AREA: Authors

MATERIALS: Student textbooks

READING/WRITING FOCUS: Students use their textbooks to locate and read about authors. Students *make author's card* for textbooks.

HOMEWORK: Make an author's card and title card for a book at home.

Recreational Reading

PRONOUNS: Locate *pronouns and their referents*.

LESSON 86

Phonics/Spelling

STRUCTURAL EMPHASIS: Suffix, *ed*

VOCABULARY EMPHASIS: Health words (parts of the body)

WRITING: Write a paragraph.

HOMEWORK: Write down ways to take care of the body.

Composition

PREWRITING: Discuss flying kites. Underline possessive pronouns in students' sample sentences on the board.

WRITING ASSIGNMENT: Write a paragraph to tell about flying kites with friends.

PROOFREADING THRUST: Use a *possessive pronoun*.

Study Skills

KNOWLEDGE AREA: Varies

MATERIALS: Card catalogue drawers or a diagram on the board showing drawers with letters on drawers

READING/WRITING FOCUS: Groups of 3–4 students work at table with 2–3 card catalogue drawers. *Find the titles*, etc., on strips. File the strip in front of the card as you find each in the drawer.

Recreational Reading

PRONOUNS. Locate *pronouns and their referents*.

LESSON 87

Phonics/Spelling

STRUCTURAL EMPHASIS: Root words

VOCABULARY EMPHASIS: Health words (the senses)

WRITING: Write paragraph or sentences. Word list—study, test, check, file.

HOMEWORK: Write about the sense you think is most important. Tell why.

Composition

PREWRITING: Discuss underwater sights. Emphasize pronouns in student sentences on the board.

WRITING ASSIGNMENT: Pretend you are underwater. Describe all the sights.

PROOFREADING THRUST: Include an *exclamatory sentence* with proper punctuation.

Study Skills

KNOWLEDGE AREA: Dewey Decimal System

MATERIAL: Nonfiction library books

Teacher explains purpose and use of call numbers.

READING/WRITING FOCUS: Choose a nonfiction topic. Find at least one book in the card catalogue relating to topic. Write *title and call number*.

Recreational Reading

PRONOUNS: Locate *pronouns and their referents*.

LESSON 88

Phonics/Spelling

STRUCTURAL
EMPHASIS: Sylla-
bles
VOCABULARY
EMPHASIS:
Health words (good
nutrition)
WRITING: Choose
some chart words
to write some rules
for good nutrition.
Test, and file.
HOMEWORK: Share
your nutrition ideas
at home. Tell about
a meal you had at
home that had good
nutritive value.

Composition

PREWRITING: Discuss a family
trip or outing.
WRITING ASSIGNMENT: Write
about some trip with a family
member.
PROOFREADING THRUST:
Begin one sentence with "My
mother and I. . ." or, "My
brother and I. . ."

Study Skills

KNOWLEDGE
AREA: Teacher's
choice
MATERIAL: Teacher's
choice
READING/WRITING
FOCUS: Teacher-
designed activity to
evaluate knowledge
of card catalogue
use.

Recreational Reading

PRONOUNS: Locate
*pronouns and their
referents.*

LESSON 89

Phonics/Spelling

STRUCTURAL EMPHASIS: Suffix, *able*.

VOCABULARY EMPHASIS: Health words (personal hygiene)

WRITING: Write a paragraph to tell about personal cleanliness using some chart words.

HOMEWORK: Find any examples at home of chart words; for example, *Gleem* toothpaste.

Composition

PREWRITING: Discuss "a big victory."

WRITING: Write a description of "a big victory." It may be true or imaginary.

PROOFREADING THRUST: Use at least one word that shows *excitement*.

Study Skills

CYCLE 17: USING THE CORRECT REFERENCE SOURCE

KNOWLEDGE AREA: Automobiles

MATERIAL: Almanac, encyclopedia, dictionary, newspaper, magazines, etc.

READING/WRITING FOCUS: Teacher and students *discuss each reference source* shown in classroom. Teacher asks questions. Which source would you choose to find answer? Students write answer. Example: 1. Where would you look to find pictures of different model cars?

2. What is a carburetor?

3. How many cars were made in 1975?

Recreational Reading

PRONOUNS Locate *pronouns and their referents*.

LESSON 90

Phonics/Spelling

STRUCTURAL EMPHASIS: Suffix, *ous*

VOCABULARY EMPHASIS: Health words (body systems—nervous, digestive, etc.)

WRITING: Use chart words to tell about any one body system. Check words to test on. Or Chart Review Test

HOMEWORK: Use your health book to find any chart words. Give page on which you find them.

Composition

PREWRITING: Discuss "Exploring a cave with my friend." Or Sharing Day

WRITING: Students write sentences about exploring caves with a friend. No pronouns allowed. Exchange papers. Then rewrite and put in pronouns wherever possible.

PROOFREADING THRUST: Check for correct *pronoun* usage.

Study Skills

KNOWLEDGE AREA: Imported automobiles

MATERIAL: Almanac, atlas, encyclopedia, newspaper, etc.

READING/WRITING FOCUS: Same as yesterday's format. Teacher asks questions, students tell where they would look for answer. Emphasize imported cars to utilize the atlas as a source. Example: When cars are imported from Germany, which ocean do they cross to get here? (use atlas)

Recreational Reading

PRONOUNS: Locate *pronouns and their referents*.

LESSON 91

Phonics/Spelling

CYCLE 3: LINGUIS-
TIC/STRUC-
TURAL EMPHA-
SIS STUDY:

WORD FOCUS: Syn-
onyms (Note:
Beginning with
Lesson 91, there is
no writing assign-
ment in this mod-
ule; however, if
time permits, the
teacher should cre-
ate a writing assign-
ment. Maximum
time should be
given for students
to locate words and
take the spelling
test.)

Composition

CYCLE 11: KINDS OF SEN-
TENCES Discuss *octopus* and
write different kinds of sentences. Proofread for correct
punctuation.

Study Skills

KNOWLEDGE
AREA: Sea animals
MATERIAL: Various
reference books
READING/WRITING
FOCUS: Read in
various reference
materials about sea
animals and *write
informative sen-
tences* based on facts
obtained from each
source.

Recreational Reading

CYCLE 11:
CAUSES,
EFFECTS, COM-
PREHENSION OF
PLOT Location of
*cause and effect
relationships*, and
*comprehension of
plot* in library
books.

LESSON 92

Phonics/Spelling

WORD FOCUS:
Antonyms

Composition

Discuss plot and write a short
story, proofreading for use of
interrogative sentence and *question mark*.

Study Skills

CYCLE 18: MAIN
IDEAS Teacher
should read list of
related words and
have students group
words and provide
appropriate categori-
cal headings. *Write
main idea heading*
with several items
under each heading.
Example: *Fruits*
Orange, Apple,
Lemon, Plum

Recreational Reading

Location of *cause and
effect relationships*,
and *comprehension
of plot* in library
books.

LESSON 93

Phonics/Spelling	Composition	Study Skills	Recreational Reading
WORD FOCUS: Homonyms	Discuss the police force and write paragraphs, proofreading for a *command sentence* with understood *you* as its subject.	Read paragraphs in health or social studies textbooks about current topic of study or nutrition and write the *main idea* of each paragraph.	Location of *cause and effect relationships*, and *comprehension of plot* in library books.

LESSON 94

Phonics/Spelling	Composition	Study Skills	Recreational Reading
WORD FOCUS: Contractions	Discuss a conversation between a paper plate and a human as preparation for writing a short story. Proofread for *comparisons* and *punctuation* (quotation marks for dialogue).	Read a fable or poem and write the *main idea* in a complete sentence.	Location of *cause and effect relationships*, and *comprehension of plot* in library books.

LESSON 95

Phonics/Spelling	Composition	Study Skills	Recreational Reading
WORD FOCUS: Compound words	Discuss *spiders* and write sentences to test partner on identifying four kinds of sentences. Proofread for unusual *adjectives* (description).	CYCLE 19: OUTLINING Read in social studies textbook about bodies of water. Use headings and subheadings to outline passage read or a chapter under study.	Location of *cause and effect relationships*, and *comprehension of plot* in library books.

LESSON 96

Phonics/Spelling

WORD FOCUS:
Three-syllable words
(emphasis on sylla-
bication)

Composition

CYCLE 12: EXPANDING SEN-
TENCES Discuss *fish* to expand
simple sentences, proofreading
for relative pronouns *who*, *that*,
and *which*.

Study Skills

Read in encyclopedia
about a famous per-
son and *outline* basic
types of information.

Recreational Reading

Location of *cause and
effect relationships*,
and *comprehension
of plot* in library
books.

LESSON 97

Phonics/Spelling

WORD FOCUS:
Four-syllable words
(emphasis on sylla-
bication)

Composition

Discuss "losing my temper" and
write a paragraph, proofreading
for expanding sentences using
adverbs.

Study Skills

Read in any reference
book about an ani-
mal. Write an *out-
line* of basic informa-
tion.

Recreational Reading

Location of *cause and
effect relationships*,
and *comprehension
of plot* in library
books.

LESSON 98

Phonics/Spelling

WORD FOCUS:
Five-syllable words

Composition

Discuss compound sentences.
Write related sentences about
"A Foggy Night" and join sen-
tences with *and*, *but*, or *or*.
Proofread for use of *comma* with
and, *but*, *or*.

Study Skills

CYCLE 20: TAKING
NOTES Read in
social studies text-
book about a country
other than your own
and *take notes* of
most important facts.
Notes need not be in
complete sentences.

Recreational Reading

Location of *cause and
effect relationships*,
and *comprehension
of plot* in library
books.

159

LESSON 99

Phonics/Spelling

WORD FOCUS:
Words with multiple
meanings

Composition

Discuss complex sentences and
write a paragraph about "The
Gloflu" (*nonsense word*), proofreading for one sentence beginning with *when*, *if*, *although*, or
after.

Study Skills

Read in newspaper any
sports story and *take
notes*. Share infor-
mation with others.

Recreational Reading

Location of *cause and
effect relationships*,
and *comprehension
of plot* in library
books.

LESSON 100

Phonics/Spelling

WORD FOCUS:
Words with multiple
meanings

Composition

Discuss "The Shrinking Student"
and write a short story, proofreading for use of one *complex
sentence*, that has *so*, *even*,
though, or *although* in it.

Study Skills

Read in science or
health textbook
about bacteria and
take notes. Share
notes.

Recreational Reading

Location of *cause and
effect relationships*,
and *comprehension
of plot* in library
books.

LESSON 101

Phonics/Spelling

WORD FOCUS:
Words with prefixes,
un, *in*

Composition

CYCLE 13: WRITING OPIN-
IONS Discuss *homework* and
write a paragraph to express
your opinion. Proofread for *reasons to support your opinion*.

Study Skills

CYCLE 21: SUMMA-
RIZING Read an
article in a magazine
on current events
and *summarize* the
main points in sen-
tences.

Recreational Reading

CYCLE 12: LOCATE
DIFFERENT
PARTS OF
SPEECH IN
LIBRARY BOOKS

Teacher and students
will locate and dis-
cuss *different parts
of speech* in library
books.

160

LESSON 102

Phonics/Spelling	**Composition**	**Study Skills**	**Recreational Reading**
WORD FOCUS: Words with prefixes, *dis, im*	Discuss responsibilities and rights at home. Write at least one paragraph and express your opinion. Proofread for *possessive pronouns*.	Read a short story in a fiction book that takes place in the autumn and *summarize* the plot.	Teacher and students will locate and discuss *different parts of speech* in library books.

LESSON 103

Phonics/Spelling	**Composition**	**Study Skills**	**Recreational Reading**
WORD FOCUS: Words with prefixes, *pre, re*	Read an editorial or discuss a local issue. Write a letter to the editor and express your *opinion*—give reasons.	Read in science and/or health textbook and *summarize* all information about the *brain*.	Teacher and students will locate and discuss *different parts of speech* in library books.

LESSON 104

Phonics/Spelling	**Composition**	**Study Skills**	**Recreational Reading**
WORD FOCUS: Words with prefixes, *sub, ex*	Discuss *honesty* and write your opinion in a paragraph. Proofread for correct use of *there, their*.	Recall a TV show and *summarize* the plot. Use beginning, middle, ending paragraphs.	Teacher and students will locate and discuss *different parts of speech* in library books.

LESSON 105

Phonics/Spelling

WORD FOCUS:
Review of any words
  with prefixes
  located in newspa-
  per or magazine

Composition

Discuss *mass communication* and
  write at least one paragraph
  expressing your opinion. Proofread for root words with *suffixes*.

Study Skills

Read in any reference
  material, choose
  topic, and take notes
  for a short *oral*
  report. Begin outline
  or written report.
  (To be completed
  tomorrow.)

Recreational Reading

Teacher and students
  will locate and dis-
  cuss *different parts
  of speech* in library
  books.

LESSON 106

Phonics/Spelling

WORD FOCUS:
Words with suffixes,
  ment, ing

Composition

CYCLE 14: CONDUCTING
  AND WRITING INTERVIEWS
  Discuss interviews and/or read
  an interview. Write *questions* to
  interview a classmate. Proofread
  for *fact* and *opinion questions*.

Study Skills

Read about topic cho-
  sen for report. Take
  notes and complete
  outline.

Recreational Reading

Teacher and students
  will locate and dis-
  cuss *different parts
  of speech* in library
  books.

LESSON 107

Phonics/Spelling

WORD FOCUS:
Words with suffixes,
  ful, ness

Composition

Read *questions* written during
  Lesson 106 to a classmate, write
  responses, rewrite as an interview in paragraphs. Proofread
  for *direct quotations* and *punctuation*.

Study Skills

Read in reference
  materials and com-
  plete gathering infor-
  mation for oral
  reports.

Recreational Reading

Teacher and students
  will locate and dis-
  cuss *different parts
  of speech* in library
  books.

LESSON 108

Phonics/Spelling	**Composition**	**Study Skills**	**Recreational Reading**
WORD FOCUS: Words with suffixes, *sion, tion*	Discuss interviewing an adult outside of class. Prepare list of questions for interview. Proofread for *subject-verb agreement.* HOMEWORK: Interview an adult using questions you wrote.	Oral report presentations. Prepare any *visuals* for report (allow 2 days).	Teacher and students will locate and discuss *different parts of speech* in library books.

LESSON 109

Phonics/Spelling	**Composition**	**Study Skills**	**Recreational Reading**
WORD FOCUS: Words with suffixes, *ly, less*	Review interview notes to write interview in paragraphs. Proofread for correct *abbreviation of titles,* Mr., Mrs., Dr., Sen., Ms., etc.	Presentation and evaluation of *oral reports* (continued) or written reports completed and proofread.	Teacher and students will locate and discuss *different parts of speech* in library books.

LESSON 110

Phonics/Spelling	**Composition**	**Study Skills**	**Recreational Reading**
WORD FOCUS: Words with irregular plural spellings. Or Chart Review Test	Discuss Christopher Columbus (or any famous person). If you could interview anyone (living or dead), who would it be? Write questions that you would ask. Proofread for *fact* and *opinion* questions. Or Sharing Day	Same as Lesson 109.	Teacher and students will locate and discuss *different parts of speech* in library books.

163

LESSON 111

Phonics/Spelling

CYCLE 4: FUNC-
TIONAL WORDS
WITH SPELLING
EMPHASIS.
VOCABULARY
EMPHASIS: Name
different careers
SPELLING EMPHA-
SIS: *ph*

Composition

CYCLE 15: TECHNIQUES IN
STORIES Discuss *exaggeration*.
Read examples from folk tales.
Write examples of exaggeration
as you read a tall tale. Proofread
for *notation of source* (character, page number).

Study Skills

CYCLE 22: FOL-
LOWING DIREC-
TIONS Read in *TV
Guide* to find *order
forms*. Cut out form
and fill in correct
information, follow-
ing directions.

Recreational Reading

CYCLE 13: CHAR-
ACTER ANALYSIS
AND RECOGNIZ-
ING FANTASY
AND REALISM
Discuss characters,
*fantasy and/or real-
ism* in library
books.

LESSON 112

Phonics/Spelling

VOCABULARY
EMPHASIS: Train-
ing needed for dif-
ferent careers
SPELLING EMPHA-
SIS: *al*

Composition

Discuss use of *comma in series*.
Write a tall tale and use technique of exaggeration. Proofread
for *superlatives*.

Study Skills

Read in magazine to
locate a recipe.
Write steps needed
to *follow directions*
in preparation.

Recreational Reading

Discuss characters,
*fantasy and/or real-
ism* in library
books.

LESSON 113

Phonics/Spelling

VOCABULARY
EMPHASIS: Safety
(bicycle and high-
way)
SPELLING EMPHA-
SIS: *ng*

Composition

Display pictures that illustrate
"Nature." Discuss "Natural
Inspiration." Write a paragraph
about a picture on display using
an example of a simile or metaphor. Proofread for *simile* or
metaphor or both.

Study Skills

Teacher reads *oral
directions* for stu-
dents to locate and
connect points on a
grid. Form simple
shapes. (Stencil a
grid sheet to use, if
necessary.)

Recreational Reading

Discuss characters,
*fantasy and/or real-
ism* in library
books.

LESSON 114

Phonics/Spelling

VOCABULARY
   EMPHASIS: Safety
   (home and school)
SPELLING EMPHA-
   SIS: *thr*

Composition

Discuss "Bubble Gum." Write a
poem or paragraph, proofreading for vivid *picture words* and/
or a *comparison*. (Simile example: like a balloon)

Study Skills

Student designs simple
shape on grid. Write
directions and give
points for drawing
your design. Give
directions to a class-
mate to follow.

Recreational Reading

Discuss characters,
*fantasy and/or real-
ism* in library
books.

LESSON 115

Phonics/Spelling

VOCABULARY
   EMPHASIS: Gov-
   ernment (national,
   people, and posi-
   tions)
SPELLING EMPHA-
   SIS: *or*

Composition

Teacher reads an opening for a
scary story or discusses mood
words. Write story "Lost in
Space" proofreading for *mood
words.*

Study Skills

CYCLE 23: MAKING
   A SURVEY Read *TV
   Guide* to list several
favorite programs.
Survey other stu-
dents to get their
first choice. Tabulate
results. Show on a
chart, listing pro-
grams from most
popular to least pop-
ular.

Recreational Reading

Discuss characters,
*fantasy and/or real-
ism* in library
books

LESSON 116

Phonics/Spelling

VOCABULARY
EMPHASIS: Government (local,
people, and positions)

SPELLING EMPHASIS: *sn*

Composition

Discuss *personification*. "I am a Smile"—write paragraphs to tell about yourself (or choose any object). Proofread for correct *plural forms of nouns*.

Study Skills

Survey students asking for favorite candy bar, song, sport, etc. (your choice). Write responses. Tabulate results. Put results on a graph entitled "Favorite sports (or other) in our room." Complete in next day's class.

Recreational Reading

Discuss characters, *fantasy and/or realism* in library books.

LESSON 117

Phonics/Spelling

VOCABULARY
EMPHASIS: Home (appliances and furniture, etc.)

SPELLING EMPHASIS: *sl*

Composition

Discuss *time words*. Write several paragraphs about "The Crystal Ball." Proofread for *time words* (examples: long ago, last year, yesterday).

Study Skills

Complete graph of survey from yesterday. Display graphs.

Recreational Reading

Discuss characters, *fantasy and/or realism* in library books.

LESSON 118

Phonics/Spelling

VOCABULARY
EMPHASIS: Home
(responsibilities and
activities)
SPELLING EMPHA-
SIS: *gh*

Composition

Discuss *emotion words*. Write at
least one paragraph—"An Angry
Me," "A Happy Me." Proofread
for *words that show emotions*.

Study Skills

CYCLE 24: VARIED
MAP SYMBOLS
Read in social stud-
ies textbook to locate
a products map.
Write statements
about the products
grown or manufac-
tured.

Recreational Reading

Discuss characters,
*fantasy and/or real-
ism* in library
books.

LESSON 119

Phonics/Spelling

VOCABULARY
EMPHASIS: Trans-
portation (land)
SPELLING EMPHA-
SIS: *tr*

Composition

Display a large art print. Record
reactions of students. Discuss
fact and *opinion*. Write sentences about picture. Label
each as F (fact) or O (opinion)
and proofread labels.

Study Skills

Design your own state
product map. Title
it. Show several
products on map.
Include a key for
symbols. Write facts
and items your state
produces.

Recreational Reading

Discuss characters,
*fantasy and/or real-
ism* in library
books.

LESSON 120

Phonics/Spelling

VOCABULARY
EMPHASIS: Trans-
portation (air,
water, etc.)
SPELLING EMPHA-
SIS: *nt*
Or Chart Review Test

Composition

Listen to a musical selection.
Write facts about the music;
write opinions. Proofread for
correct use of *a*, *an*, *the* (articles). Or Sharing Day

Study Skills

Use a social studies
textbook or encyclo-
pedia and read a
population and/or
rainfall map. Write
factual statements
based on each map.

Recreational Reading

Discuss characters,
*fantasy and/or real-
ism* in library
books.

LESSON 121

Phonics/Spelling

VOCABULARY
EMPHASIS:
Health care
SPELLING EMPHA-
SIS: *spl*

Composition

Discuss one purpose of an author:
to entertain. Write one paragraph having "to entertain" as
the purpose—suggestion, "snap,
crackle, pop." Proofread for
comma series.

Study Skills

CYCLE 25: STUDY
SKILLS DIVER-
SITY Look in maga-
zines (or fiction
books). Choose a pic-
ture to observe for 5
minutes. Write all
you recall about the
picture. Check for
main points and
details. Study skill—
*observing and
reporting.*

Recreational Reading

CYCLE 14: LOCAT-
ING SOCIAL
STUDIES INFOR-
MATION
PREFIXES, SUF-
FIXES   Students
locate social studies
information, pre-
fixes, and suffixes
in library books.

LESSON 122

Phonics/Spelling

VOCABULARY
EMPHASIS: Com-
munication
SPELLING EMPHA-
SIS: *spr*

Composition

Discuss author's purpose: to
inform or give information.
Write a paragraph and tell
"How to be a good bike rider."
Proofread for use of *time words*
or *sequence*.

Study Skills

Read catalogues and
write a list of items
needed for a camp-
ing trip. Fill out an
order. Study Skill—
filling out forms and
making judgments.

Recreational Reading

Locate social studies
information, pre-
fixes, and suffixes
in library books.

LESSON 123

Phonics/Spelling

VOCABULARY
EMPHASIS: Citi-
zenship
SPELLING EMPHA-
SIS *nk*

Composition

Discuss description as an author's
purpose. Write a paragraph,
poem, or several sentences to
describe Superman (or other
character). Proofread for *adjectives* and *adverbs*.

Study Skills

Read in science text-
books about frogs,
tadpoles, or butter-
flies. Write ques-
tions and ask a part-
ner to check for main
facts. Study Skill—
locating main ideas.

Recreational Reading

Locate social studies
information, pre-
fixes, and suffixes
in library books.

LESSON 124

Phonics/Spelling

VOCABULARY
  EMPHASIS: Civil
  preparedness in
  disasters
SPELLING EMPHA-
  SIS: *em*

Composition

Discuss persuasion techniques.
Design an advertisement using
words or phrases to persuade
someone to buy a product.
Proofread to locate *words of
persuasion*, "loaded words,"
such as *always*, *never*.

Study Skills

Read in atlas (or ency-
clopedia) to locate
information on the
population of several
states. Make com-
parison statements
about population
information. Study
Skill—making com-
parisons.

**Recreational
Reading**

Locate social studies
information, pre-
fixes, and suffixes
in library books.

LESSON 125

Phonics/Spelling

VOCABULARY
  EMPHASIS: Shop-
  ping (clothing
  stores, etc.)
SPELLING EMPHA-
  SIS: *nd*

Composition

CYCLE 16: ELEMENTS OF A
STORY   Discuss a "Desert
Trip." Write a short story.
Proofread for an accurate setting
description.

Study Skills

Discusss energy con-
servation. Read and
observe in maga-
zines. Cut out exam-
ples of unnecessary
and necessary appli-
ances. Study skill—
making judgments.

**Recreational
Reading**

Locate social studies
information, pre-
fixes, and suffixes
in library books.

LESSON 126

Phonics/Spelling

CYCLE 5: RECREA-
TIONAL WORDS
WITH STRUC-
TURAL EMPHA-
SIS

VOCABULARY
EMPHASIS: Team
sports

STRUCTURAL
EMPHASIS: Plu-
rals formed with *s*
and *es*

Composition

Discuss sequence of plot. Write
about, "The Life of a Drop of
Water." Proofread for correct
sequence and *paragraph organi-
zation*.

Study Skills

Read weather maps in
newspaper to record
high and low tem-
peratures on a
graph. Study Skill—
using a map, graph-
ing information.

Recreational Reading

Locate social studies
information, pre-
fixes, and suffixes
in library books.

LESSON 127

Phonics/Spelling

VOCABULARY
EMPHASIS:
Movies

STRUCTURAL
EMPHASIS: Suffix,
er

Composition

Discuss a popular athlete and
write a character description.
Proofread to include *physical
actions*, and *personality traits*.

Study Skills

Read in science text-
book about planets.
Draw a diagram of
the solar system
showing location,
size, etc., or write
information you find
associated with
planets. Study
Skill—using dia-
grams for informa-
tion, associating
information with a
topic.

Recreational Reading

Locate social studies
information, pre-
fixes, and suffixes
in library books.

171

LESSON 128

Phonics/Spelling	Composition	Study Skills	Recreational Reading
VOCABULARY EMPHASIS: Television STRUCTURAL EMPHASIS: Nouns made plural by adding *s*	Discuss *reality and fantasy*. List real and imaginary items. Write sentences. Use one real and one fantasy word in each sentence. Proofread for use of *to, two, too*.	Read in a comic book and select a story. Write a *summary* of the story. Study skill—summarizing.	Locate social studies information, prefixes, and suffixes in library books.

LESSON 129

Phonics/Spelling	Composition	Study Skills	Recreational Reading
VOCABULARY EMPHASIS: Water activities STRUCTURAL EMPHASIS: Suffix, *ed*	Discuss writing a conclusion to a story. The teacher or students read part of a story. Students write a conclusion. Proofread for *verb usage*.	Read teacher-chosen material or science fiction story to *separate fact and opinion* statements. List each. Study skill—fact and opinion.	Locate social studies information, prefixes, and suffixes in library books.

LESSON 130

Phonics/Spelling	Composition	Study Skills	Recreational Reading
VOCABULARY EMPHASIS: Games STRUCTURAL EMPHASIS: Suffix, *able* Or Chart Review Test	Discuss "Lost at the Zoo." Write half of a story. Exchange with a partner who writes the conclusion. Proofread for sentence beginning with *when, if*, or *because*. Or Sharing Day	Read in health textbook about accident prevention. Write *cause and effect statements* (or lists). Study skill—recognizing cause and effect.	Locate social studies information, prefixes, and suffixes in library books.

LESSON 131

Phonics/Spelling

VOCABULARY
  EMPHASIS: Boats
STRUCTURAL
  EMPHASIS: Pre-
  fixes, *be, de*

Composition

CYCLE 17: TIME-LAPSE WRIT-
ING Discuss "Shipwrecked."
Begin a long story. Proofread
for *setting description* in the
story.

Study Skills

Read in magazines to
find brand name
words with multiple
meanings. Use the
words to write sen-
tences showing dif-
ferent meanings.
(Example: *Dawn* is a
detergent. I got up
at *dawn*.) Study
skill—multiple
meanings.

Recreational Reading

CYCLE 15: IDENTI-
FYING SEN-
TENCE STRUC-
TURE Students
locate simple, com-
pound, and com-
plex sentences.

LESSON 132

Phonics/Spelling

VOCABULARY
  EMPHASIS:
  Reading
STRUCTURAL
  EMPHASIS:
  Adding *er, est* to
  adjectives

Composition

Time-Lapse writing continued—
"Shipwrecked." Add a character. Proofread for *character
description*.

Study Skills

Read in science and/or
health textbooks
about blood, listing
main words. Use the
glossary to help
pronounce and
define words. Study
skill—use of glossary
and main words as
clues.

Recreational Reading

Identify sentence
structure.

LESSON 133

Phonics/Spelling	Composition	Study Skills	Recreational Reading
VOCABULARY EMPHASIS: Bicycles and motorcycles STRUCTURAL EMPHASIS: Root words	Time-lapse writing continued. Add an animal. Proofread for *sound, emotion* and *mood* words (sensory imagery).	Read a state map making a list of main cities, use letters to show location. Study skill—map reading, using a grid.	Identify sentence structure.

LESSON 134

Phonics/Spelling	Composition	Study Skills	Recreational Reading
VOCABULARY EMPHASIS: Games or activities to do alone STRUCTURAL EMPHASIS: Compound words	Time-lapse writing continued. Add an object to the story. Proofread for *sentence fragments*.	Read part of a short story about weather in a fiction book. Predict what will happen. Write your prediction. Read to check. Study Skill—predicting.	Identify sentence structure.

LESSON 135

Phonics/Spelling

VOCABULARY
EMPHASIS: Clubs
or organizations
(4-H, Scouts,
NBA, NCAA, etc.)
STRUCTURAL
EMPHASIS:
Abbreviations

Composition

Time-lapse writing continued
Add a happy event and conclu-
sion. Proofread for *run-on sentences*.

Study Skills

Read in social studies
textbook (and/or
encyclopedias) about
earthquakes, writing
down *cause and
effects*. Study skill—
cause and effect.

Recreational Reading

Identify sentence
structure.

LESSON 136

Phonics/Spelling

VOCABULARY
EMPHASIS: Sports
equipment
STRUCTURAL
EMPHASIS: Suffix,
ure

Composition

CYCLE 18: OTHER FORMS OF
WRITING Read in class a short
fable. List the characters and
write a sentence to describe
each. Proofread for *conjunc-
tions*.

Study Skills

Read in telephone
book and list several
different *abbrevia-
tions* (in listings and
yellow pages), and
their meanings.
Study skill—under-
standing abbrevia-
tions.

Recreational Reading

Identify sentence
structure.

LESSON 137

Phonics/Spelling	Composition	Study Skills	Recreational Reading
VOCABULARY EMPHASIS: Seasonal games (winter and summer games, or choose one sport) STRUCTURAL EMPHASIS: Compound words	Read in class a fable or fables. Write the lesson each fable teaches. Proofread for *subject/verb agreement*.	Read in science textbook about reptiles (or other topic under study). Work with partner. Read 15 minutes. Write all you remember. *Compare with partner* and check. Study skill—recall of main idea and details.	Identify sentence structure.

LESSON 138

Phonics/Spelling	Composition	Study Skills	Recreational Reading
VOCABULARY EMPHASIS: Vacations (trips, places, activities, etc.) STRUCTURAL EMPHASIS: *ing* form of verbs	Read and discuss a fable. Write a fable. Proofread for *plurals*.	Read in *TV Guide* making a list of programs with present, past, or future settings. Study skill—recognizing historical sequence.	Identify sentence structure.

LESSON 139

Phonics/Spelling

VOCABULARY
EMPHASIS: Arts,
crafts, and hobbies
STRUCTURAL
EMPHASIS: Suffix,
less

Composition

Read a tall tale. Write any examples of *exaggerated language*
used. Proofread for *correct
spelling*.

Study Skills

Read in fiction books to
find examples of fact
and opinion. Write
your examples and
briefly explain.
Study skill—recog-
nizing fact and opin-
ion.

Recreational Reading

Identify sentence
structure.

LESSON 140

Phonics/Spelling

VOCABULARY
EMPHASIS: Sports
position—player
words (any sport:
quarterback, guard,
referee, forward).
Or Chart Review
Test
STRUCTURAL
EMPHASIS: Divi-
sion of words into
syllables

Composition

Discuss tall tales. Write a tall tale.
Proofread for *exaggerated language*. Or Sharing Day

Study Skills

Read a city map and
write clear directions
from point X to point
Y, using directional
words (N, E, S, W).
Study skill—map
skills, following
directions.

Recreational Reading

Identify sentence
structure.

LESSON 141

Phonics/Spelling

CYCLE 6: EXPAND-ING VOCABU-LARY WITH SPELLING EMPHASIS Locate and list unfamiliar words in news-papers

SPELLING EMPHA-SIS: *ph* (Unfamiliar words put on the chart do not have to have the *ph* spelling emphasis in them. Chart should contain both words designated by students as unfa-miliar to them, *and* words containing the *ph* spelling.)

Composition

Read a play to discuss play form. Write a short play. Proofread for *characters* and *setting*.

Study Skills

Read in any material to find any information you can relate to pol-lution. Explain the relationship. Study skill—relating infor-mation.

Recreational Reading

CYCLE 16: LOCAT-ING SCIENCE INFORMATION AND FIGURA-TIVE LANGUAGE Locate science information and recognize figurative language in library books.

LESSON 142

Phonics/Spelling

Locate unfamiliar words in *Time*, *Newsweek*, and other magazines.

SPELLING EMPHA-SIS: *ve*

Composition

Complete play. Add necessary stage or speaking directions. Proofread for proper *dialogue form*. Rewrite for homework.

Study Skills

Read in music books about holiday songs, finding examples of sensory imagery. List the phrase/sense. Study skill—recognizing sensory imagery.

Recreational Reading

Locate science infor-mation and recog-nize figurative lan-guage in library books.

LESSON 143

Phonics/Spelling

Locate unfamiliar words in music textbooks.

SPELLING EMPHASIS: *ry*

Composition

Discuss any popular song lyric. Students write a song (title open). Proofread for use of *incorrect pronoun* or *verb tense* usage.

Study Skills

Read in newspaper to locate display ads and classified ads. Cut out an example of each. Compare and contrast. Describe purpose of each. Study Skill—making comparisons.

Recreational Reading

Locate science information and recognize figurative language in library books.

LESSON 144

Phonics/Spelling

Locate unfamiliar words in newspapers.

SPELLING EMPHASIS: *rt*

Composition

Present songs and/or plays to the class. Discuss writings.

Proofread for *rhyme* and *emotion words*.

Study Skills

Read in a magazine and choose several pictures showing outdoor scenes. Describe the main idea of each picture in one sentence. Study skill—main idea.

Recreational Reading

Locate science information and recognize figurative language in library books.

LESSON 145

Phonics/Spelling

Locate unfamiliar words in *TV Guide* or other magazines.
SPELLING EMPHASIS: *ff*

Composition

CYCLE 19: WRITING BOOK REPORTS Discuss a favorite fiction book. Write a letter to a friend recommending the book. Proofread for words or phrases that *excite reader's curiosity*.

Study Skills

Read in a science textbook about bees. Relate information on how bees are helpful to man (how harmful?). Study skill—relating information.

Recreational Reading

Locate science information and recognize figurative language in library books.

LESSON 146

Phonics/Spelling

Locate unfamiliar words in newspaper.
SPELLING EMPHASIS: *iz*

Composition

Discuss "Fame." Write a poem about a famous person you have read about. Proofread for *adjectives*.

Study Skills

Read in social studies textbook using maps and index to locate information about rivers. Make a list of rivers and write information found on maps and in reading. Study skill—map reading and locating details.

Recreational Reading

Locate science information and recognize figurative language in library books.

LESSON 147

Phonics/Spelling

Locate unfamiliar words in social studies textbook.
SPELLING EMPHA-SIS: *wn*

Composition

Discuss opinions and write a book review. Proofread for *opinion words*.

Study Skills

Read in mathematics textbook locating key words in problems about money. Write the *key words* that are clues to the operations needed to solve problems. (Example: total = addition) Study skill—key words to main idea.

Recreational Reading

Locate science information and recognize figurative language in library books.

LESSON 148

Phonics/Spelling

Locate unfamiliar words in *Time, Newsweek*, other magazines.
SPELLING EMPHA-SIS: *rc*

Composition

Discuss book covers. Design a book jacket for a book you have read. Proofread for *title, author, spelling, capital letters*.

Study Skills

Read in magazines to find pictures related to seasons. Cut and paste pictures. Write a list of the clues in the picture that suggest a season. Study skill—making inferences.

Recreational Reading

Locate science information and recognize figurative language in library books.

LESSON 149

Phonics/Spelling

Locate unfamiliar
  words in news-
  paper.
SPELLING EMPHA-
  SIS: *em*

Composition

Continue book jacket project.
  Write plot information inside
  the book jacket. Proofread for
  adverbs or *prepositions*.

Study Skills

Read in newspaper to
  find examples of arti-
  cles that
1. give information
2. entertain
3. describe
4. persuade.
Classify articles accord-
  ing to author's intent
  by making class chart
  on the board. Study
  skill—recognizing
  author's intent.

Recreational Reading

Locate science infor-
  mation and recog-
  nize figurative lan-
  guage in library
  books.

LESSON 150

Phonics/Spelling

Locate unfamiliar
  words in telephone
  book.
SPELLING EMPHA-
  SIS: *rk* Or Chart
  Review Test

Composition

CYCLE 20: SITUATION WRIT-
  ING Discuss "Winning a Mil-
  lion Dollars." Write a short
  story. Proofread for use of suffixes, *tion, sion*. Or Sharing Day

Study Skills

Read in telephone
  book and study
  emergency symbols.
  Draw the symbols—
  study. Test with a
  partner to recognize
  the symbols and
  explain the relation-
  ship. Study skill—
  symbolism.

Recreational Reading

Locate science infor-
  mation and recog-
  nize figurative lan-
  guage in library
  books.

LESSON 151

Phonics/Spelling	Composition	Study Skills	Recreational Reading
Locate unfamiliar words in spelling textbook. SPELLING EMPHASIS: *po*	Discuss "Teachers." Write a poem in which you are the teacher. Proofread for words to express *emotions*.	Read poetry in poetry collections and find examples of similes and metaphors. Write down lines containing comparisons. Study skill—recognizing similes and metaphors.	CYCLE 17: WORD DEFINITION IN CONTEXT Students locate and discuss unfamiliar words in library books using context clues to understand meanings.

LESSON 152

Phonics/Spelling	Composition	Study Skills	Recreational Reading
Locate unfamiliar words in *Time*, *Newsweek*, other magazines. SPELLING EMPHASIS: *dy*	Discuss "If I had Three Wishes." Write paragraphs. Proofread for *topic sentence* for each paragraph and capital *I*.	Read in science textbook about meteors. *Summarize* information. Study skill—summarizing.	Word definition in context.

LESSON 153

Phonics/Spelling	**Composition**	**Study Skills**	**Recreational Reading**
Locate unfamiliar words in newspaper. SPELLING EMPHASIS: *gth*	Discuss "Fortune Tellers." Begin a short story using a fortune teller as one of the characters (two-day time-lapse writing). Proofread for a *simile* or *metaphor*.	Students read in science textbooks about amphibians. Teacher questions. Students write answers to recall details. Check. Study skill—recall details.	Word definition in context.

LESSON 154

Phonics/Spelling	**Composition**	**Study Skills**	**Recreational Reading**
Locate unfamiliar words in language textbook. SPELLING EMPHASIS: *mb*	Complete story begun in lesson 153. Draw a picture to illustrate. Proofread for description of a *conflict* and its *resolution*.	Read area code map in telephone book. List several cities. Determine area code for each and write it down. Study skill—map skills.	Word definition in context.

LESSON 155

Phonics/Spelling

Locate unfamiliar words in *Time*, *Newsweek*, or other magazines.

SPELLING EMPHASIS: *syn*

Composition

Discuss "Being Caught in a Fire." Write a short story. Proofread for *cause* and *effect* in the plot.

Study Skills

Read help wanted ads in the newspaper and write down unfamiliar words in any ad you choose. Try to guess the meaning from the information available. Use a dictionary to check. Study skill—word definition in context.

Recreational Reading

Word definition in context.

LESSON 156

Phonics/Spelling

Locate unfamiliar words on food/house products labels.

SPELLING EMPHASIS: *hy*

Composition

Discuss "Transportation in 2000." Write paragraphs to describe what transportation would be like in the year 2000. Proofread for sentence beginning with *if* or *when*.

Study Skills

Read in any material for information you can relate to *First Aid*. Write down findings. Study skill—relating information.

Recreational Reading

Word definition in context.

LESSON 157

Phonics/Spelling	**Composition**	**Study Skills**	**Recreational Reading**
Locate unfamiliar words in newspaper. SPELLING EMPHASIS: *iv*	Discuss "Changing myself." If I could change, I would be ———. Write two paragraphs about physical changes, and one paragraph about personality changes. Proofread for use of suffixes, *er, est*.	Read in social studies textbook or encyclopedia about railroads and write conclusions about how railroads have affected life in the U.S. Study skill—forming conclusions.	Word definition in context.

LESSON 158

Phonics/Spelling	**Composition**	**Study Skills**	**Recreational Reading**
Locate unfamiliar words in science textbook. SPELLING EMPHASIS: *mp*	Discuss "Wild Horses." Write about an adventure with a wild horse. Proofread for use of *contractions*.	Read in magazine to locate advertisements showing *techniques of persuasion*. Cut out ad and explain persuasive technique. Study skill—recognizing techniques of persuasion.	Word definition in context.

LESSON 159

Phonics/Spelling	**Composition**	**Study Skills**	**Recreational Reading**
Locate unfamiliar words in encyclopedias. SPELLING EMPHASIS: *nt*	Discuss "If I were an automobile, I'd be . . ." Write a paragraph to tell what make you'd be and why. Describe your life. Proofread for affix, *ing*.	Teacher reads beginning of a story. Students listen and *predict conclusion*. Write prediction. Share. Study skill—making predictions.	Word definition in context.

LESSON 160

Phonics/Spelling	**Composition**	**Study Skills**	**Recreational Reading**
Locate unfamiliar words in *Time*, *Newsweek*, other magazines. SPELLING EMPHASIS: *eye* Or Chart Review Test	Discuss "Thank You" letters. Write a thank you note to someone for something nice they have done for you. Proofread for *commas* in letter parts. Or Sharing Day	Read in health textbook about bacteria. Teacher asks questions and students write factual information they recall. Study skill—recall details.	Word definition in context.

LESSON 161

Phonics/Spelling

Locate unfamiliar words in newspaper.

SPELLING EMPHASIS: *cy*

Composition

CYCLE 21: PARTS OF SPEECH REVIEW Discuss "Secret Formula X-19." Write short story or paragraph. Proofread for all proper *adjectives* and *nouns*.

Study Skills

Read in any material to find information you can relate to physical fitness. List your findings. Study skill—relating information.

Recreational Reading

CYCLE 18: DRAWING CONCLUSIONS Teacher questions students about possible conclusions or inferences they might make from reading material.

LESSON 162

Phonics/Spelling

Locate unfamiliar words in mathematics textbook.

SPELLING EMPHASIS: *ap*

Composition

Discuss "An Embarrassing Episode in My Life." Write paragraphs to explain. Proofread to locate all *verbs*, present and past tense.

Study Skills

Read in mathematics textbook or map in telephone book about *time zones*. Make a chart to show time differences or make statements—"When it is 8:00 a.m. in New York, it is ———in San Francisco." Study skill—map skills, analogy.

Recreational Reading

Drawing conclusions and inferences in library books.

LESSON 163

Phonics/Spelling

Locate unfamiliar
words in dictionary.
SPELLING EMPHA-
SIS: *tw*

Composition

Discuss "The Stillygull" (or other
nonsense word). Write a
description of the word. Locate
all *adjectives* and *adverbs*.

Study Skills

Read teacher-designed
multiple-choice
materials to choose
the correct word
meaning. Write the
meaning to show it
fits in the context of
the sentence. Study
skill—word defini-
tion in context.

Recreational Reading

Drawing conclusions
and inferences in
library books.

LESSON 164

Phonics/Spelling

Locate unfamiliar
words in *Time*,
Newsweek, other
magazines.
SPELLING EMPHA-
SIS: *rl*

Composition

Discuss "The Smart Pill." Write a
short story. Proofread for all
pronouns and their referents.

Study Skills

Read in social studies
textbook and use the
index to locate infor-
mation about moun-
tains. Write one *fact*
from each page in
index. Study skill—
using an index, locat-
ing details.

Recreational Reading

Drawing conclusions
and inferences in
library books.

LESSON 165

Phonics/Spelling

Locate unfamiliar words in fiction books.

SPELLING EMPHASIS: *sis*

Composition

Discuss "The Gold Snail." Write a short story or poem. Proofread for all *prepositional phrases*.

Study Skills

Read list of words by teacher which may suggest *symbols* (students can add to list). Draw a symbol and name an object that conveys the idea of the word. Example:

word	*symbol*	*object*
love		valentine
luck		4-leaf clover (or horseshoe)

Study skill—detecting symbolism.

Recreational Reading

Drawing conclusions and inferences in library books.

LESSON 166

Phonics/Spelling

Locate unfamiliar words in newspaper. Use 12 words from Lessons 141 and 153 and alphabetize.

SPELLING EMPHASIS: *sne*

Composition

CYCLE 22: TIME-LAPSE WRITING Discuss different mystery stories. Describe the setting and introduce a main character. Proofread for *compound sentences*.

Study Skills

Read in magazines and/or newspapers to locate symbols (esp. in advertising logos). Cut out the *symbol* and write what it symbolizes. Study skill—symbolism.

Recreational Reading

Drawing conclusions and inferences in library books.

LESSON 167

Phonics/Spelling

Locate unfamiliar words in health textbooks.
SPELLING EMPHASIS: *url*

Composition

Time-lapse continued. Add a mysterious event. Proofread for possessive *pronoun* and *noun forms* and *exclamation point*.

Study Skills

Read in magazine to select a picture showing an outdoor activity involving people. Write your *interpretation* of what is happening and how the people feel. Study skill—inferences.

Recreational Reading

Drawing conclusions and inferences in library books.

LESSON 168

Phonics/Spelling

Locate unfamiliar words in magazines or *TV Guide*.
SPELLING EMPHASIS: *flo*

Composition

Time-lapse continued. Add a fantasy character or event. Proofread for *prepositional phrases*.

Study Skills

Read in any material to relate information to oceans. Try to include more than one material. Write findings. Study skill—relating information.

Recreational Reading

Drawing conclusions and inferences in library books.

LESSON 169

Phonics/Spelling	Composition	Study Skills	Recreational Reading
Locate unfamiliar words in spelling textbook. SPELLING EMPHASIS: *opt*	Time-lapse continued. Proofreading thrust: *interrogative pronouns*: *who, what, which* at beginning of sentence. Add scientific information (either true or unrealistic).	Read in social studies book about historical events. Arrange in sequence of time. Study skill—event sequence.	Drawing conclusions and inferences in library books.

LESSON 170

Phonics/Spelling	Composition	Study Skills	Recreational Reading
Locate unfamiliar words in newspaper. SPELLING EMPHASIS: *eg* Or Chart Review Test	Time-lapse continued. Present a reasonable solution and write a conclusion. Proofread for all *punctuation marks*. Or Sharing Day	Design a map of a park area. Include a *key* to show your symbols. Study skill— map skills and symbols.	Drawing conclusions and inferences in library books.

LESSON 171

Phonics/Spelling	Composition	Study Skills	Recreational Reading
Locate unfamiliar words in fiction books. SPELLING EMPHASIS: *cyc*	CYCLE 23: WRITING IN A JOURNAL Staple together sheets and cover to make a *journal*. Discuss that a journal is for writing down your feelings, ideas, opinions. Write about a friend. Proofread for *positive descriptive words*.	Read in any material and find information relating to computers. List your related information. Study skill—relating information.	CYCLE 19: LOCATING MATHEMATICS AND/OR HEALTH INFORMATION Students read in library books to locate mathematics and/or health information.

LESSON 172

Phonics/Spelling

Locate unfamiliar words in science textbook.
SPELLING EMPHA-SIS: *exp*

Composition

Discuss "Today I am." Write in your journal an opinion on any topic. Proofread for *pronouns*.

Study Skills

Read in magazines to locate food ads. Design a satirical food ad. (Discuss satire. Study skill—recognizing satire.

Recreational Reading

Locate math and/or health information in library books.

LESSON 173

Phonics/Spelling

Locate unfamiliar words in news-papers.
SPELLING EMPHA-SIS: *ght*

Composition

Discuss family members. Write in your journal about one family member. Proofread for at least one *comma series*.

Study Skills

Read/skim stories in short story collections to find examples in which author's purpose is
1. to inform
2. to describe
3. to entertain
4. to persuade.
Study skill—recognizing author's intent.

Recreational Reading

Locate math and/or health information in library books.

LESSON 174

Phonics/Spelling

Locate unfamiliar words in encyclopedias.
SPELLING EMPHA-SIS: *spa*

Composition

Write in your journal about early childhood memories (good and/or bad). Proofread for use of demonstratives *this, that, these, those*.

Study Skills

Plot your spelling test scores for a period of time on a graph. Study skill—graphing information.

Recreational Reading

Locate math and/or health information in library books.

LESSON 175

Phonics/Spelling

Locate unfamiliar words in *Time*, *Newsweek*, or other magazines.

SPELLING EMPHA-SIS: *zu*

Composition

Write in your journal your feelings about your school year. Proof-read for correct use of *do*, *did*, *does*, *done*.

Study Skills

Read rate charts in telephone book and make statements that compare costs with different times, direct-dialing, opera-tor assistance. Study skill—reading charts.

Recreational Reading

Locate math and/or health information in library books.

LESSON 176

Phonics/Spelling

Locate unfamiliar words in social studies textbook.

SPELLING EMPHA-SIS: *bom*

Composition

CYCLE 24: WRITING AN AUTOBIOGRAPHY Class makes an outline for an auto-biography. (Two-day writing cycle.) Proofread for *important items* in outline.

Study Skills

Read in any material to find information relating to insects. Make list of findings. Study skill—relating information.

Recreational Reading

Locate math and/or health information in library books.

LESSON 177

Phonics/Spelling

Locate unfamiliar
  words in poems.
SPELLING EMPHA-
  SIS: *hyp*

Composition

Autobiography, continued. Complete your autobiography.
  Proofread for correctly written
  dates, cities, states.

Study Skills

Read in newspaper to
  find food advertise-
  ments and make
  comparisons for wise
  consumerism. List
  item, different costs,
  which store you
  would go to. Study
  skill—comparisons,
  judgments.

Recreational Reading

Locate math and/or
  health information
  in library books.

LESSON 178

Phonics/Spelling

Locate unfamiliar
  words in news-
  papers.
SPELLING EMPHA-
  SIS: *nst*

Composition

Discuss school activities this year.
  Write about your favorite school
  activity this year. Proofread for
  paragraph structure.

Study Skills

Read words and analo-
  gies prepared by
  teacher to associate
  words and ideas and
  to form own analo-
  gies. Example:
1. salt and ————.
2. toes are to foot as
fingers are to ————.
  Study skill—analo-
  gies, associations.

Recreational Reading

Locate math and/or
  health information
  in library books.

LESSON 179

Phonics/Spelling	Composition	Study Skills	Recreational Reading
Locate unfamiliar words in dictionaries. SPELLING EMPHASIS: *ric*	Discuss "Best Book I Read All Year." Write a book report. Proofread for *reasons* to support your *opinions*.	Read in newspaper or magazines to locate recipe. List measurement words, ingredients. Alphabetize each list. Study skill—classifying, alphabetizing.	Locate math and/or health information in library books.

LESSON 180

Phonics/Spelling	Composition	Study Skills	Recreational Reading
Locate unfamiliar words in magazines. SPELLING EMPHASIS: *apo* Or Chart Review Test	Discuss "Summer Fun." Write a letter to your teacher telling of your summer plans. Use correct letter form. Proofread for *commas*. Or Sharing Day	Read in any material to find information relating to hair. Explain the relationship. Study skill—relating information.	Locate math and/or health information in library books.

Checklist for Teachers, Other Educators, and Visitors

The following are selected important items that you should initiate as soon as possible after starting the *Success* program.

_____ 1. Post a schedule of the time each module is taught outside the classroom door.

_____ 2. Display charts containing some of the students' vocabulary in the room each day.

_____ 3. Keep a variety of reading materials in the classroom.

_____ 4. Individualize instruction within *each* of the four modules each day.

_____ 5. Include comprehension and word analysis questions within *each* module each day.

_____ 6. Set up boxes of folders containing student daily writings from the Phonics/Spelling, Composition, and Study Skills Modules.

_____ 7. Do not stereotype groups of students.

_____ 8. Have students keep records of library books read.

_____ 9. Acknowledge positively work completed by students in each module.

_____ 10. Use at least one proofreading thrust included in the Composition Module each day.

_____ 11. Give homework each day.

_____ 12. Have each student take at least one library book home each night—a book he or she has selected.

_____ 13. Be sure students have immediate access to dictionaries.

_____ 14. Encourage students to *think* in each module.

_____ 15. Use professional initiative to develop the *Success* program.

_____ 16. Avoid having students memorize words, including lists of sight words.

_____ 17. Inform parents of the *Success* program.*

_____ 18. Invite parents and other interested persons to visit the classroom.

_____ 19. Correlate writing, spelling, speaking, and listening instruction with reading instruction.

_____ 20. Help students decode unknown words as they are encountered in a variety of printed materials.

_____ 21. Begin the first three modules with a few minutes of whole-class instruction and work with individuals at their desks for the remainder of these modules.

_____ 22. Exchange library books frequently.

_____ 23. Teach all four modules within each lesson.

_____ 24. Ask volunteers to sit beside a student and help that student in completing parts of the module under way.

*See Anne H. Adams, *Success in Beginning Reading and Writing* (Santa Monica, Calif.: Goodyear, 1978), chapter nine.

___ 25. Combine both structure and flexibility in teaching students to read any words they encounter, and to want to read more.

___ 26. Have students date and file their own papers each day in the Phonics/Spelling, Composition, and Study Skills Modules.

Index